BASEBALL

THE NEW YORK GAME

How the National Pastime
Paralleled US History

Tony Morante

Foreword by Michael Kay

Published by 9 INCH Marketing

Editing by Lee Heinrich, layout by Amit Dey, and cover by Joshua Vaughan

ISBN: 978-1-952234-10-1

First Printing: 2021
Printed in the United States of America

Baseball The New York Game is available for bulk orders. For further details and special pricing, please e-mail: yanktony@gmail.com or call 917 902 6231

Proceeds to benefit The Bronx County Historical Society

*This book is dedicated to the memory of my mom
and dad, Ann & Tony, and to Marcia,
my one and only.*

Praise For
Baseball The New York Game

"Tony Morante was our team historian and our legendary tour guide for my entire 16-year career in pinstripes. He was as much a true Yankee as anyone in the organization. In his one-of-a-kind tours, Tony took you on a lot more than just leading you to the attractions and landmarks at Yankee Stadium. Along the way, he took you on a journey through time with his anecdotes and parallels of our national pastime to the history of this great country. Now, Tony has linked the history of the United States with the game of baseball in this extraordinary work. I invite you to take Tony's latest and greatest tour by reading his wonderful history lesson *Baseball The New York Game*.

— **Bernie Williams,**
16-year centerfielder of the New York Yankees

"For many years Tony Morante was the passionate and affable man responsible for giving fans tours of Yankee Stadium. In *Baseball The New York Game* Morante takes readers on a different type of tour as he digs deep to explain how baseball history and American history are endlessly linked. This is a riveting book that would appeal to baseball fans, American history buffs, and anyone interested in taking an exciting baseball-rich tour through these pages."

—**Jack Curry-**
YES Network analyst for YANKEE games.
New York Times best-selling author of *Full Count:
The Education of a Pitcher* with David Cone
and *The Life You Imagine* with Derek Jeter

"When it comes to the history of baseball, its relationship with New York, and its impact on American history, nobody knows it better than Tony Morante. Tony has a unique ability to make history come alive. His superb storytelling and genuine affection for the game of baseball can be felt with every word he writes."

—Ryan Ruocco-Yankees and Nets Play
by Play broadcaster for YES Network.
NBA and WNBA PBP broadcaster for ESPN;
Boxing PBP broadcaster for DAZN.

"As the mother of two teenagers, I have recognized over the years how history isn't a focus of the youth of today. There are so many things going on in the world that they have failed to recognize the importance of understanding how we got to the place we are today. Introducing baseball, something they love, to teach them about history will allow them to understand how their favorite pastime helped to shape our history."

—Denise Kuhbier MS, RN, LNHA, CCM
Advanced Aging Life Professional Alzheimer's
Association, Board of Director

"As a student of history, and a baseball aficionado, and a born and raised New Yorker, one of my most memorable baseball moments was attending the first game played at Shea Stadium following the September 11 catastrophe. Major League baseball played an important healing role in that national moment. I was proud to be in attendance."

—Stephen J. Beninati
- First Vice President | Senior Portfolio Manager,
Portfolio Focus | Financial Advisor

"Our administration, staff, and community have worked extensively with Tony Morante over the years on the numerous levels of engagements of his project, *Baseball The New York Game.* The project has evolved from building a cohesive community support program for low-income families to growing a massive initiative around attendance improvement and academic supports. We are grateful for Mr. Morante's steadfast commitment to our vision around changing and impacting lives in the Bronx and throughout NYC and look forward to supporting and growing his passion toward community influence and engagement."

—Frank Cutrone,
Community School Director,
United Community Schools- UFT,

"There is a need and an urgency for students in the United States to learn about the history of our country. Tony Morante's book serves as an excellent resource for teachers to use in accomplishing that goal. Through a chronological presentation of U.S. history, Mr. Morante illustrates how baseball has been a major influence in bringing us together as Americans. His narrative demonstrates how baseball has been a key factor in influencing U.S. history and American culture. History and baseball intertwine throughout the pages of this book."

—Dr. Guy Stella,
Retired Superintendent,
Woodbridge, CT

"As a young man, Tony Morante literally trod the hallowed grounds upon which stood *The House That Ruth Built*, as he escorted Mickey Mantle from Center Field to the Yankees dugout at the end of games. The author *knows* Baseball; the author *feels* Baseball. In this book, the reader will not only get the "facts and figures" of our National Pastime but will also be drawn into the heart and soul of America's game. Lovers of the game will deepen their understanding of the relationship between the growth of our Nation and the evolution of Baseball. This book is for the serious fan."

—Father Gabriel B Costa, Ph D;
Department of Mathematical Sciences,
United States Military Academy; Department
of Mathematics and Computer Science, Seton Hall University

"Tony Morante, who established and ran Yankee Stadium tours for decades, always had a passion for the early days of New York City baseball. Now, he's directed that passion into a book which takes us back to that time long before exit velocity and streaming video. Buckle up."

--Marty Appel,
author of *Munson, Pinstripe Empire*
and *Casey Stengel*

"Baseball is the background music of America. Baseball, the perfect game, is our dream repository, it is part of who we are, the fabric that knits us together, filled with cultural landmarks that punctuate our lives that surely resonate. Tony has done a magnificent job weaving that history into the tapestry of American life."

—Ed Randall,
Host, Ed Randall's Talking Baseball,
WFAN-Radio; Host, Remember When, Sirius/XM Radio

"Who better to write *The New York Game* than Bronx-bred Tony Morante? The author uses the game of baseball to take the reader on a tour of not just New York but of the history of America as the game and the city intersect. I can't think of a better guide."

—Glenn Stout,
author, editor or ghostwriter of more than 90 books
including Author of *Yankees Century* and *The Selling of The Babe*

"Some European observers of America state that if you wish to truly understand the country, you must understand baseball. Tony Morante has now provided an account of the connection between the history of the sport and the development of the nation. He illustrates the importance of the national pastime in times of crisis, global conflict, and peaceful domestic pursuits. Starting in the nineteenth century, leisure and exercise evolved into fraternities and organized sport, especially baseball, that intertwined with America's ongoing history and contributed to the growth of the country's popular culture."

—Lloyd Ultan,
Professor of History at Fairleigh Dickinson University
and Bronx Borough Historian

"*Baseball The New York Game* is the ultimate story of the ultimate sport of baseball and how it mirrors American history. There is no better way to learn about the history of our great country than through the history of our greatest sport. And there is no better way to read it than from one of the true icons and legends in the mighty New York Yankees organization, my pal, Tony Morante!"

—Joe Piscopo,
an American comedian, actor, musician,
writer, a radio talk show host, and a regular
in the early days of Saturday Night Live

There is a need and an urgency for students in the United States to learn about the history of our country. Tony Morante's book serves as an excellent resource for teachers to use in accomplishing that goal. Through a chronological presentation of U.S. history, Mr. Morante illustrates how baseball has been a major influence in bringing us together as Americans. His narrative demonstrates how baseball has been a key factor in influencing U.S. history and American culture. History and baseball intertwine throughout the pages of this book.

—Dr. Guy Stella,
Retired Superintendent, Woodbridge, CT

"I was the Fordham University Baseball coach for the greater part of my career, The lessons the game has taught us are relevant in all aspects of our lives, which make us who we are today, proud and productive citizens. In my time as coach, I have always striven to instill those values in our young men."

—Nick Restaino

"So many Americans have enjoyed watching and playing baseball over the years. It is woven into our history and has served valuably in helping our nation heal during difficult times. There is no better baseball historian than Tony Morante to take us on a behind the scenes tour as to the impact baseball has had on the American and global culture."

—Ron Karr

"As a student of history, and a baseball aficionado, and a born and raised New Yorker, one of my most memorable baseball moments was attending the first game played at Shea Stadium following the September 11 catastrophe. Major League baseball played an important healing role in that national moment. I was proud to be in attendance."

—Stephen J. Beninati
- First Vice President | Senior Portfolio Manager,
Portfolio Focus | Financial Advisor

"As an educator, I find this would be a wonderful resource to make history a little bit more interesting to those who find it to be boring. Tony

Morante has been able to tie baseball to the important dates in our country's history."

—Blanca Restaino,
Teacher-Wolfpit School, Norwalk CT 06851

"This is a clear, concise, and insightful book on the history of baseball and our pop culture . . . informative and interesting . . . reflects [the author's] baseball background and long career as the Director of Tours at Yankee Stadium."

—John Houston

Table of Contents

c. The Pitching Revolution

d. Modifications

e. Diversity

f. MLB Globalization

g. Health Issues

h. Museums

Foreword

If the history of the United States since the early 19th century is a quilt, then the game of baseball would be a thread that runs throughout the fabric. Much of the ebb and flow of America is mirrored by those of the great game. In fact, some of the low points in our nation's history were turned upward with the help of baseball.

The importance of the game of baseball is perhaps best illustrated in the aftermath of the attacks of September 11, 2001. There is perhaps no greater illustration of the resiliency of this country than President George Bush, standing proud and determined on the mound at Yankee Stadium before Game 3 of the World Series between the Yankees and the Diamondbacks at Yankee Stadium in the Bronx, just weeks after planes flew into the World Trade Center and took nearly 3,000 lives. With the entire world watching and an air of tension in the sellout crowd, President Bush stood tall, his eyes looking up into the crowd, his body covered in kevlar to guard against an attack and a phalanx of security people in the crowd and standing on the surrounding buildings making sure of the Commander in Chief's safety as well as the lives of the 55,000-plus in attendance.

Bush took a deep breath, looked toward Todd Greene, the Yankees backup catcher squatting behind home plate and delivered a perfect strike. The crowd erupted, in exultation and relief. With one pitch, Bush sent a message that we would not be deterred from living our life and this country would come back from the ugly unprovoked attacks.

On that night, the power of baseball was evident. The country needed something to latch on to, something to return to normalcy, and the President's defiant strike made everything seem a bit closer to the way it used to be and the way we wanted it to be.

This book by Tony Morante will explore how the history of the game is intertwined with American history, contributing to popular culture as we know it. Tony, who has taught social studies courses at Fordham University and at middle schools throughout his beloved borough of the Bronx, uses New York City as the focal point in the connection between the game and our nation's history over the past 200 years. He examines as how the growth of urban development paralleled the growth of baseball in those same areas, thus having an undeniable effect on our country's popular culture.

Also explored in this fine work, is how the development of train travel and the telegraph -- —for you younger readers, that is essentially a very slow email or text message ---— in the 1830s and 1840s helped sell the game to the entire country. Most importantly, during this time, New York City became the center of the universe in all things, including entertainment and finance and that only helped baseball, which was clearly becoming the national pastime.

The connection between the game and the country continues into the 21st century. It has helped the US through major heartache and setbacks and the hope is it continues to do just that through the troubling times of today.

Baseball has been the mirror the country has held up to his its collective mouths to see how it was breathing. So far, it has been the perfect inhaler, helping in times of stress and high concern. This book examines the marriage between the National Pastime and the nation that passes its time watching it.

— Michael Kay, June 2020

Former baseball journalist Michael Kay is the television play-by-play broadcaster of the New York Yankees and host of CenterStage on the YES Network, and the host of The Michael Kay Show heard on WEPN-FM in New York City and simulcast on ESPN Xtra on XM Satellite Radio.

Note of Explanation

BASEBALL *The New York Game* is organized as a linear narrative of facts and events that marries America's illustrious history with the rich background of baseball, our national pastime, beginning in the early nineteenth century until the present. The narrative includes many watershed moments that illustrate the importance of baseball during many crises and global conflicts, including the aftermath of September 11, 2001. The reader will integrate concepts that are offered to promote an ongoing discourse of our country's popular culture. One will witness how leisure and exercise evolved into the structure of fraternities and the formation of an organized sport that became the national pastime. In addition, following the main body of the text is an article on the military in baseball. This is the story of how American history and baseball intertwined as an integral part of our popular culture.

Acknowledgments

I would like to thank all who inspired, supported, and provided feedback for this book: Without the assistance of Bob Heinisch I do not know how I possibly could have completed this project . . . my right hand, to say the least. Friend and author, Marty Appel, provided guardrails throughout the project. Greg Mazzoni who helped fill in parts of my early life that were important to the introduction. The Bronx Historian, Prof. Lloyd Ultan lent his expertise in the entire editing process . . . a shocking experience for this nubile naive author. Major League Baseball Historian, John Thorn, whose early critique was invaluable. Friend and colleague, Rob Brown, for his support throughout the process. Thanks to Roe Mercora who I partnered with to develop this program. I am also indebted to the Bronx County Historical Society (BCHS) CEO, Dr. Gary Hermalyn, for his support in availing the resources of the BCHS. Thanks to Linda Tribuzio in helping the manuscript's early editing. Thanks to John Rudio who gave me a platform in the book's seminal stage. Thanks to Ernestine Miller with the NYC Casey Stengel Chapter of SABR, (Society for American Baseball Research), who helped to develop the idea for this project through its formative stages. Cecila Tan, editor for SABR, who devoted her time to review the manuscript. Colleague Brian Richards who helped to plant the seed for this book. Nicholas Sette, Major League Baseball, (MLB), Analytics, who provided invaluable insight to the current trend in recognizing the importance of analytics in baseball. Friend and colleague Rick Cerrone who assisted in bringing the importance of the media to the book. Negro Baseball Historian, John Holway, who provided the background on the Negro National League's integration of major league baseball. John Horne, National Baseball Hall of Fame, whose resources helped to illustrate the national pastime. And, of course, my family, who gave me constant inspiration!

Introduction

It all started for me on November 5, 1942, in New York City, more specifically, in the Bronx, New York, where I still live. I am the son of Anthony and Antoinette Morante, who are the children of Italian immigrants. Their parents, Carmine Morante and Anastasia Mesisco, came from Avellino and Apice in la Provincia di Benevento, Italy. My family—and by this I include my parents, sisters, grandparents, uncles, aunts, and cousins—all settled in the Little Italy section of the Bronx, centered around the legendary Italian-American enclave known as Arthur Avenue.

The Bronx was founded by Swedish settler, Jonas Bronck, and named after the Bronx River in 1639. From the bluffs of Spuyten Duyvel (Spouting, Spewing, or Spinning Devil) where the Harlem and Hudson rivers intersect in the northwest Bronx, Dutch Colonial Governor Peter Stuyvesant kept a watchful eye out for invading British ships. Another body of water, Long Island Sound, gave rise to The Riviera of New York, Orchard Beach, and City Island in the east, where families enjoyed the sun and surf on hot summer days. The Bronx encompasses 42 square miles and has a population today of nearly 1.5 million people of varied ethnicities.

The Belmont section of the Bronx is bordered by Fordham Road to the north and by 180th Street to the south, Bronx Park to the east and Third Avenue to the west with Arthur Avenue as its hub. During Stuyvesant's day, the area was farmland. By the time I came along, it was mostly an Italian-American neighborhood filled with family, friends, food, culture, language, tradition, and love. As children, we learned the ways of our ancestors from the old country. We learned the importance and love of family, of togetherness, of sharing, and of a culture dating back generations. We learned respect. We learned loyalty and honor. We learned the meaning of life in a few square blocks of tenement apartment buildings.

As Italian-Americans, we heard our heritage booming in song from vacuum tube radios and RCA Victrolas from Puccini to Sinatra to Perry Como to Dion and the Belmonts—and don't leave out vital links in the chain: Tony Bennett, (Anthony Dominick Benedetto), Louis Prima, Domenico Modugno, Vic Damone, and Jerry Vale. Our Bronx brethren were movie stars (Lauren Bacall, Tony Curtis, Anne Bancroft [Anna Maria Luisa Italiano]); entertainers (Carl Reiner, Rob Reiner, Chaz Palmentieri, Joey Bishop, Robert Klein, Bobby Darin, Jennifer Lopez); politicians (General Colin Powell, Associate Justice Sonia Sotomayor, Bella Abzug, Ed Koch, Bess Myerson, Oliver Kopell); musicians and composers (Arturo Tuscanini, Eydie Gorme, Jerry Wexler, Phil Spector); writers (Edgar Allen Poe, James Baldwin, Mary Higgins Clark). All these artists, as well as the beginning of the "Hip-Hop" generation called the Bronx home at some point during their lives. Even the pride of Long Island, Billy Joel, born in the Bronx as was the long-time Hall of Fame (HOF) voice of the Brooklyn/Los Angeles Dodgers, Vin Scully, former Dodgers' owner, Walter O'Malley, also studied at Fordham University, and current Yankees' broadcaster, Michael Kay, studied at Fordham University, as did NFL Hall of Fame Coach, Vince Lombardi, who was also a guard on the Bronx school's "Seven Blocks of Granite."

Our neighborhood was a stone's throw away from the Bronx Zoo and The New York Botanical Garden. Hundreds of churches and places of worship across many denominations and faiths were scattered throughout the Bronx. There are over 440 public schools in the Bronx, including mine, PS 59 on 182nd Street and Bathgate Avenue. Roosevelt High School and Fordham University are just a few blocks away on Fordham Road (190th Street) and Bathgate Avenue. Imagine that in a two-block radius one can start in kindergarten and finish with a college degree. Mass transportation was no problem with three bus lines, the Third Avenue El, and the D-Train all within walking distance. But why would you want to leave the Bronx? We had it all.

As kids in school, playing and getting into harmless mischief on the streets of Bathgate and Arthur Avenue, we certainly had our share of heroes. But to me, and many other Italian-American Bronx boys, none were of greater legend than Yogi Berra, Phil Rizzuto, Vic Raschi, Billy Martin and, of course, Joe DiMaggio. Sure, these New York Yankee stars hailed from all over the country, but they were ours. They played in the Bronx, the House That Ruth Built, the Green Cathedral, the Mecca of outdoor Sports and other significant events—Yankee Stadium. They were our Bronx Bombers. Soon Yankee Stadium would become my home away from home.

I learned about baseball by listening to Mel Allen, Russ Hodges, and Red Barber on the radio, reading Red Foley, Joe Trimble, Phil Pepe, and Dick Young in the newspapers, and later by watching games on a black and white television set in the living room. My dad, who was an usher at Yankee Stadium at the time (his uniform jacket resides in the Baseball Hall of Fame in Cooperstown as does my entire uniform) took me to my first Yankee game when I was six years old. I recall vividly the experience of walking through a tunnel onto the upper deck of the Stadium to an opening that produced beautiful blue skies with big white clouds, the aromas of the hot dogs, peanuts, popcorn, Cracker Jacks, beer, and other drinks that the vendors were hawking, and, of course, the perfectly manicured lush green grass. As a Bronx boy up until this point, all I had seen of the game was on that black and white television screen. What a memorable experience it was, and I was awestruck and smitten.

This was not what I saw on TV. It was in living color! The grass was greener than any grass I had ever seen. The green seats enveloped the stadium under the backdrop of that beautiful sky. The blue pinstripes and the famous blue interlocking NY logo on the pristine pinstriped uniform with the white interlocking NY on the blue caps were all laid out right there in front of me.

I was part of the crowd that roared for every Yankee hit, and screamed for every run they scored. The fans who were rooting for the home team were now friends. I was addicted for life. I wanted to learn as much as I could about baseball (I later became a member of the New York City Chapter of the Society of American Baseball Research), about New York and the Bronx, and about the nation and baseball's relation to our pop culture. As an Adjunct Professor at Fordham University, I had the honor of teaching the course of what the book, BASEBALL The New York Game is all about. And now, in the autumn of my life, I would like to share what baseball has given me. Take me out to the ballgame once more. This time, you come, too.

Why Baseball?

Historian Jacques Barzun said:

"Whoever wants to know the heart and mind of America had better learn baseball."

James H. Billington, Librarian of Congress for nearly three decades, stated in *Baseball Americana*:

We can learn a lot about America by looking at baseball. The development of leisure, sports and fitness, entertainment, publishing, consumerism, national advertising, transportation, communications, industrial archaeology, the growth of cities, the cult of celebrity, and the influence of popular culture are just some of the topics scholars will find relevant to the history of baseball in the United States. No sport has ever been as popular or as deeply entrenched in our shared past and our collective memory.

Steven Gelber wrote in his book, *Our Game*:

Baseball is a game that replicated and legitimized the social and intellectual environment of the workplace. In its orderly inning-by-inning progression, its synthesis of teamwork with individual achievement and expression, its increasing emphasis on numbers for measuring both collective and personal performance, and its corporate competitive framework (involving teams, associations, and eventually leagues), baseball was especially suited to the young American male working in a professional or business occupation."

Poet laureate, Walt Whitman offered,

It's our game! That's the chief fact in connection with it: America's game: has the snap, go, fling, of the American atmosphere---belongs as much to our institutions, fits into them significantly, as our constitutions, laws: is just as important as the sum total of our historic life.

An unnamed baseball fan puts it eloquently:

I am a fan who anxiously awaits the arrival of spring as I awaken from my winter hibernation. I embark on the season's annual journey through the spring and summer months, watch and enjoy 30 teams play the game of baseball. I celebrate the wins and grieve all the losses and hope to see my favorite team play in the coveted post (fall) season. Baseball, the game I love and revere, is our national pastime, and is the soul that has resonated deeply into the history of our nation. Throughout my childhood and into my adult years, I have an excessive and single-minded zeal for the game. The age of technology and the advent of social media outlets enables me to be kept apprised of every at bat of the game.

PART ONE

CHAPTER 1

Post-Revolutionary War Era

> a. The Cotton Gin and the Compact of 1802
>
> b. Leisure and Exercise
>
> c. Commercialization and the Market Revolution
>
> d. Urbanization and Industrialization
>
> e. The Origin of Ball Games: Town Ball to Organized Baseball

The Cotton Gin and the Compact of 1802

Before the Revolutionary War, southern plantations in America revolved primarily around tobacco, sugar, rice, and cotton. These businesses struggled for the most part in the aftermath of the War for Independence until 1793, when Eli Whitney invented the cotton gin. Though a tremendous boon to the agriculture industry, there was a price to pay for this great innovation. The downside of the success of "king cotton" came with the brutal expansion of the cotton fields and the desire for development. The Compact of 1802 forcibly removed Native Americans by clearing paths from the southeastern states west to today's Oklahoma. The burden of this injustice thrust on the backs of Indian nations such as the Creek, Choctaw, Cherokee, Chickasaw, and Seminoles ignited slavery. (1). Another forceable removal of the Indian Nation came about in the 1830s, when President Andrew Jackson fostered what came to be known as the "Trail of Tears".

Whitney also developed interchangeable mechanical parts, spurring on the Industrial Revolution through manufacturing and mass production. It was a commercialization that led to the emergence of the Market Revolution, which helped to open wide the industrialization era. The cycle, in its most simplistic form, was that the South grew the cotton on the backs of slaves and sold it to the North where the great textile mills manufactured the fabric needed for the country's growth. Population growth and the improvement in transportation helped mushroom the markets and that opened the door to capitalism. (2) So, ascribing to this theory, it would seem to be against their own interests for most Northerners to be in favor of abolition. Yet it proved to be far more complicated.

Leisure and Exercise

Baseball's rise is purely up for conjecture. A new world opened to the citizenry as the people continued to recover from the War of Independence's ravages and veer away from the Puritan legacy that condemned sports. Games of "ball" began to establish more structure in the early 1800s.

While these folk games of ball grew in popularity, there was a shift from an agrarian society to an urban community. (3) To understand the true origins of the game, let us take on a leisure and exercise game, which precipitated the game's evolution.

"Base Ball", as we know it, had various roots. As early as 1744, John Newbery reported a game played in his book, *A Little Pretty Pocket-Book.* Then, in 1777, General George Washington felt that his troops needed an escape from the dangers of war and the boredom of camp. As Elliot Gorn and Warren Goldstein wrote in their book, *A Brief History of American Sports,* "He urged his officers to promote exercise and vigorous amusements among their troops, improve all the leisure time your brigades may have from other duties in maneuvering and teach the men the use of their legs which is of infinitely more important than learning the manual exercise... Games of Exercise may not only be permitted but encouraged."

After the Revolutionary War, the United States government advocated leisure and exercise, including original games of "ball" to help the citizenry recover from the doldrums of the war's aftermath. After that, games of ball were played in Pittsfield, Massachusetts in 1791—and likely earlier—in a document as discovered by Major League Baseball historian John Thorn and former Major League pitcher Jim Bouton. (4)

The Commercialization and the Market Revolution

The Market Revolution, which began around 1800, precipitated a series of changes. The transformation occurred when most Americans saw more significant opportunities by leaving the countryside of the agrarian society and moving to the cities to work in factories, thus setting the tone for urbanization. "The market revolution occurred as a result of sweeping economic, cultural, and political changes that took place between the American Revolution and the Civil War and affect how we live today," as stated in Study.com. (5) Important factors precipitated by the Revolution:

- The agricultural explosion in the South and West and the textile boom in the North strengthened the economy in complementary ways.
- Eli Whitney's cotton gin and pioneering work with metal mechanical parts contributed significantly to industrialization.
- Large-scale domestic manufacturing, concentrated in the North, decreased dependence on imports and increased wage labor.
- The federal government's power grew under influential Kentucky Congressman, House Speaker, and Secretary of State Henry Clay's

American System, which led to many improvements in the form of expanded roadways and canal systems.

- The rapid development and westward expansion during the Market Revolution resulted in land speculation, which caused economic boom and bust. (6)

By 1820, the United States was moving toward the forefront of urbanization. Cities expanded into open fields as commerce burgeoned. Sporting fraternities began to evolve from the simple folk games into a more organized form of town ball. The Lower East Side of New York City grew rapidly as the Market Revolution increasingly drew more merchants and businesses there.

Urbanization and Industrialization

Robert Fulton established the first commercial steamboat, which traveled up and down the Hudson River in New York in 1807. Soon after, steamboats took over the waters of both the Mississippi River and the Ohio River.

In 1811, a commission appointed by the New York City Legislature laid out the famous street grid pattern for New York City. The city grew northward by leaps and bounds. Yet this clean design later thwarted ballplayers' opportunity to establish a place for their baseball games in Manhattan, continually pushing the location of the early games of ball into real estate prime for development.

The opening of the Erie Canal in 1825 further contributed to urban growth during the Market Revolution. The canal quickly became the primary conduit to the West. It was followed in 1828 by construction of the Baltimore and Ohio Railroad, the first public railroad in the United States. Urbanization energized the development of sport as the cities underwent a rapid rate of growth. It became the primary reason for the development of organized sport and athletic pastimes in America. (7) Through the next decade, hundreds of steamboats moved up and down western rivers carrying manufactured goods and people. Shortly after that, base ball became more of an organized game. The northeastern cities of Philadelphia, New York, Brooklyn, and Boston in the United States, plus Beachville in Ontario, Canada, all became hotbeds for the game. In *City Games: The Evolution of American Urban Society and the Rise of Sports,* Steven A. Riess wrote,

> **Clean sport provided sedentary workers a substitute for the slow pace of life by improving health, morals, and character. Men who subscribed to this ideology were sporting gentlemen—respectable individuals who believed in hard work, planning for the future, and leading Christian lives. Their favorite sports, such as baseball, were moral, personally uplifting, and socially functional. (8)**

The earliest documented evidence of the origins of the game played in New York was at a staged match to draw patrons to a saloon known as Jones' Retreat, located around Broadway and 8th Street. George Thompson who stated that baseball emerged gradually, not by invention reported in the *New York Times* in 2001, the following article written anonymously in the *National Advocate* newspaper on April 25, 1823:

> **I was last Saturday much pleased in witnessing a company of active young men playing the manly an athletic game of "base ball" at the Retreat in Broadway (Jones'). I am informed they are an organized Association, and that a very interesting game will be played on Saturday next at the above place, to commence at half past 3 o'clock P.M. Any person fond of witnessing this game may avail himself of seeing it played with consummate skill and wonderful dexterity.... It is surprising, and to be regretted that the young men of our city do not engage more in this manual sport; it is innocent amusement, and healthy exercise, attended with but little expense, and has no demoralizing tendency. (9)**

While base ball was still in its developmental stages, the country witnessed the advent of the railroad. The railroad's growth provided a connection that allowed baseball and American history to establish a formidable relationship. Then, in 1844, Samuel F.B. Morse introduced long-distance communications in the form of the telegraph. Wiring of the transmitter paralleled the tracks laid by the railroad. It is hard to picture telegraph wiring without train tracks in the same scenario. These cultural and technological advances became a significant part of the Industrial Revolution and furthered the spread of base ball.

The Origin of Ball Games/Town Ball to Organized Baseball

Philadelphia and Camden N.J., reported organized games as early as 1831. The New York Gotham Base Ball Club came together in 1837 with the first set of bylaws. Known as the "New York, or Gotham, or Magnolias, or Washington clubs from the 1830s through the 1860s, these clubs were lineally the same, and appear to have gone by several names at the same time," as stated in *Base Ball Founders.* (10) In 1838, games of ball were also being played in Beachville, Ontario, Canada. There was no specific date that the original term "base ball" unified to "baseball." Still, we know "base ball" was used in the latter part of the nineteenth century; after that, the term became commonly referred to as "baseball."

So, who were the "founders" of this game? Until recently, two prominent names linked baseball's origins. Abner Doubleday was the first. Doubleday, a career soldier, ordered the first shots fired by the Union in defense of Fort Sumter that commenced the Civil War. He fought in the titanic battles at Antietam, Bull Run, and Gettysburg, ending the war with major-general rank. Upon his death in 1893, nothing in his obituary mentioned anything about the game he would be eternally linked. (11) It was while Doubleday was a cadet at the United States Military Academy in 1839 that he was retroactively—and erroneously—credited as the "founder of base ball." (This fabrication was fostered by former pitcher and sporting goods magnate Albert Goodwill Spalding in a commission that he set up in 1905).

The second touted "founder" of the game was Alexander Joy Cartwright, a New York City bank teller who served as a volunteer fireman. Cartwright was an instrumental member in the forming of the Knickerbockers. And, later on, through a great publicity campaign by his heirs, he was claimed to have been the "true" founder of baseball since he was a leader of the "Knickerbocker Fire Company" and proffered the rules of the "Knickerbocker Game." Most of the credit Cartwright received fell short of reality. Cartwright later received a plaque in his honor in the Baseball Hall of Fame. (12)

William R. Wheaton and Doc Adams were two gentlemen who were very involved with the game in its early stages of development. From a letter in a San Francisco newspaper in 1887, former original Gotham/Knickerbocker, William R. Wheaton, also considered a "father of base ball," wrote in a letter published in a San Francisco newspaper:

In the '30s, [*sic*] I lived at the corner of Rutgers Street and E Broadway in New York. I was admitted to the bar in '36 and was very fond of physical exercise.... There was a racquet club in Allen Street with an enclosed court. Myself and intimates, young merchants, lawyers, and physicians, found cricket too slow and lazy a game. We couldn't get enough exercise out of it. Only bowler and batter had anything to do, and the rest of the players might stand around all afternoon without getting a chance to stretch their legs. Racket was lively enough, but it was expensive and not in an open field where we could have a full swing and plenty of fresh air with a chance to roll on the grass. Three-cornered cat was a boys game and did well enough for slight youngsters, but it was a dangerous game for powerful men, because the ball is thrown to put out a man between bases, and it had to hit the runner to put him out....

We had to have a good outdoor game, and as the games then in vogue didn't suit us we decided to remodel three-cornered cat and make a new game. We first organized what we called the Gotham baseball club. This was the first ball organization in the United States, and it was completed in 1837.... Among the members were doctor John Miller, a popular physician of that day; John Murphy, a well-known hotel-keeper; and James Lee, president of the New York Chamber of Commerce.... The first step we took in making baseball was to abolish the rule of throwing the ball at the runner and order that it should be thrown to the baseman instead, who had to touch the runner with it before he reached the base.... During the regime of three-cornered cat there were no regular bases, but only such permanent objects as a bedded boulder or an old stump, and often the diamond looks strangely like an irregular polygon. We laid out the ground at Madison Square [*sic*] in the form of an accurate diamond, with home plate and sandbags for bases. You must remember that what is now called Madison Square [*sic*], opposite the Fifth Avenue Hotel, in the thirties was out in the country, far from the city limits. We had no short-stop, and often played with only six or seven men on a side. The scorer kept the game in a book we had made for that purpose, and it was he who decided all disputed points. The modern empire and his tribulations were unknown to us....

After the Gotham club had been in existence for a few months, it was found necessary to reduce the rules of the new game to writing. This work fell to my hands, and the code I then formulated is substantially that in use today. We abandoned the old rule of putting out on the first bound and confined it to fly catching. The Gotham played a game of ball with the star Cricket Club of Brooklyn and beat the Englishman out of

sight, of course. That game and the return were the only two matches ever played by the first baseball club. (13)

The earliest recorded rules of a baseball game in the United States were written by Wheaton on September 23, 1845. The first recorded baseball game was played on October 6, 1845, at Elysian Fields, in Hoboken, New Jersey. (14) The first match game that incorporated the Knickerbocker bylaws came on June 19, 1846, between the New York Ball Club and the New York Knickerbockers—the New York Nine defeated Cartwright's Knickerbockers.

Overall, Americans continued to enjoy the combination of athletics and social life during the formative years of team sports. Although the game did help to provide a sense of fraternity and cohesion that was lacking in mid-nineteenth-century America, at times, it contributed to further contention and fragmentation. George Kirsch, in his book, *Baseball and Cricket: TheCreation of American Team Sports,* summarized the transformation of leisure time into organized baseball:

America's earliest amateur clubs aimed to provide healthful recreation and promote goodwill among players, and to a considerable extent, they succeeded. However, they could not escape the athletic and social tensions inherent in competition. While the goal was "friendly strife," each contest's aim was a victory; winning was joyous while defeat was bitter. In cities that were diverse in religion, nationality, and economic class, inter-club rivalries inevitably involved personal, social, and athletic conflicts. (15)

As the culture of New York was responding to urbanization, so too was the outlook on sports. In *Our Game,* author Charles Alexander quoted Melvin Adelman: "Baseball fulfilled the sporting universe's requirements created by the changing social and urban environment in the antebellum period." (16)

CHAPTER 2

Organized Base Ball

---

a. Gotham
b. The Knickerbocker (New York) Rules
c. Organized Baseball/Gambling
d. Manifest Destiny/Annexation of Texas
e. The Gold Rush

Gotham

Gotham became the nickname for the first organized New York City baseball club in 1837. The name came from Washington Irving when he affixed the nickname "Gotham"—an Anglo-Saxon word meaning "Goat's Town"—to New York City in 1807. Irving also supplied the nickname of "Knickerbocker" for the team that was an offshoot of the term "Gotham". This name came from his satirical book, *The History of New York from the Beginning of the World to the End of the Dutch Dynasty,* surreptitiously written under the pen name Diedrich Knickerbocker in 1809 when Irving dedicated the book to The New York Historical Society. By this time, almost all of New York City's written records had either been destroyed in the Revolutionary War or in the Great Fire of 1776 that burned some 500 houses on the Lower West Side of the city. (1)

1845-The Knickerbocker (New York) Rules

On September 23, 1845, the New York Knickerbocker Base Ball Club tweaked the New York Gotham rules to create their own set of playing rules and bylaws. Following are the 20 rules that resulted in the language and terminology of the day:

1. **Members must strictly observe the time agreed upon [for] exercise (the game) and be punctual in attendance.**

2. **When assembled for exercise, the President, or in his absence, the Vice President, shall appoint an Umpire, who shall keep the game in a book provided for that purpose, and note all violations of the Bylaws and Rules during the time of exercise.**

3. **The presiding officers shall designate two members as Captains, who shall retire and make the match to be played, observing at the same time that the players put opposite each other should be as nearly equal as possible; the choice of sides should be then tossed for, and the first in hand [the leadoff hitter] to be decided in like manner.**

4. **The bases should be from home to second base, forty-two paces; from first to third base, forty-two paces, equidistant.**

5. **No stump match [exhibition games] shall be played on a regular day of exercise.**

6. **If there should not be a sufficient number of the Club present at the time agreed upon to commence exercise, gentlemen not members may be chosen in to make up the match, which shall not be broken up [halted] to take in members that may afterward appear; but, in all cases, members should have the preference, when present, at the making of the match.**

7. If members appear after the game commenced, they may be chosen in if mutually agreed upon.

8. The game to consist of twenty-one counts or aces [runs], but at the conclusion, an equal number of hands must be played.

9. The ball must be pitched, and not thrown, for the bat.

10. A ball knocked out [of] the field, or outside the range of first or third base. is foul.

11. Three balls struck and missed, and the last one caught, is a hand-out; if not caught is considered fair, and the striker bound to run. [If the third strike was a tipped ball caught by the catcher it was considered a hand out.]

12. If a ball is struck, and tipped, and caught, either flying or on the first bound, it is a hand out.

13. A player running the bases shall be out if the ball is in the hands of an adversary on the base, or the runner is touched with it before he makes his base, it being understood, however, that in no instance is a ball to be thrown at him.

14. A player running who shall be preventing an adversary from catching or getting the ball before making his base is a hand out.

15. Three hands out, all out.

16. Players must take their strike in regular turn.

17. All disputes and differences relative to the game, to be decided by the Umpire, from which there is no appeal.

18. No ace or base can be made on a foul strike.

19. A runner cannot be put out in making his base when a balk is made by the pitcher.

20. However, one base allowedwhen a ball bounds out of the field when struck.

The Knickerbockers played the first game under these rules on October 6, 1845. (2)

Coverage of this rapidly growing sport was in the hands of the bustling New York press, which became the prime means of reporting the game's events. With the advancements that developed by way of the telegraph and with improvements in typesetting and mass mailings, the New York press was able to spread the word of the New York game far and wide. Eventually, the Philadelphia and Massachusetts games of "town ball" relented to the more organized "New York" game. "The evolution of the city, more than any other single factor, influenced the development of organized sport and recreational athletic pastimes in America," stated Steven A. Riess, in *City Games: The Evolution of American Urban Society and the Rise of Sports.* (3)

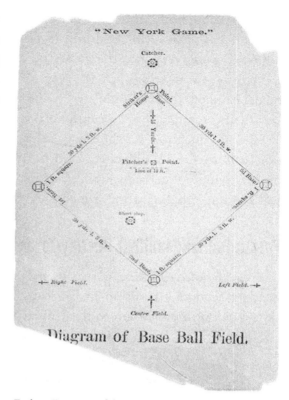

Earliest Diagram of the "New York Game" playing field
Courtesy - Library Of Congress

Gambling

During the early 1840s, two groups of fraternities began to organize. The first group was the "sporting fraternity" for those who enjoyed sports, including light competition, with social gatherings following the contests. The "baseball fraternity," however, organized strictly for playing base ball. Associations and clubs were then forming with rules, appointed officials, and scheduled matches. (4) Until this point, the game was played for healthful recreation and the merriment that followed. However, once the games became organized, the fans who wanted to spur interest started to wager on the outcome and, at times, predetermined the outcome by "fixing" or "hippodroming," which eventually escalated into corruption.(5)

Oddly enough, it was gambling that gave the game an added dimension as it attracted a different crowd to this fledgling sport—gamblers. Thus, a symbiotic relationship formed between the two entities of base ball and the gambling world, which provided additional revenue.

Potato Famine/Manifest Destiny/Texas

The Great Potato Famine started in Ireland in 1845, followed shortly after by economic hardship in Germany. This led to the first significant waves of immigration to the United States. At this time, the term

The Angel Columbia: This 1872 painting, "American Progress," depicts Columbia as the "Spirit of the Frontier," carrying telegraph lines across the western frontier to fulfill manifest destiny. (6)
Courtesy - Library of Congress

"Manifest Destiny," which significantly impacted the country, was first used to speak about the mindset for the push for westward expansion. President James K. Polk encouraged the population to seek, explore, and settle the country west of the Mississippi River.

Manifest Destiny led to the annexation of Texas in1845. Soon after that, Britain and the U.S. agreed to extend the western border, which settled a longstanding dispute with Great Britain over ownership of the Oregon territory (the future states of Oregon, Washington, Idaho, and Montana) and set the current boundary between the United States and Canada.

After the Mexican-American War formally ended in 1848, Mexico agreed to a treaty that established the Rio Grande as the border between Texas and Mexico, giving the New Mexico and California territories to the United States, at a cost of $15 million. This newly possessed land included what is now California, Nevada, Utah, most of New Mexico, Arizona, and parts of Colorado and Wyoming. (7) However, there was a high cost. Manifest Destiny, while a boon to the economy, became a terrible strain on the Native-American Indians as they were, once again, displaced from their land, causing many altercations. Thus, starting with

The New York Knickerbockers introduced the first uniform in 1849.
The above image is that of the Knickerbockers and the Excelsiors
Courtesy - Hall of Fame

the Louisiana Purchase in 1803, Manifest Destiny wiped out cultures, leaving a lasting negative effect on many of those who had called North America their home. (8)

The Gold Rush

In 1848 gold was discovered in Sutter's Mill in California, resulting in the massive rush of people searching for a quick fortune out West. So began California's introduction to baseball. Men who knew the game from the streets of New York helped bring the game to the gold fields. As author Kevin Nelson explained in *The Golden Game: The Story of California Baseball*, "'Wagon-tongue' bats... derived their name from the old-fashioned bats cut from the tongues and axletrees of farm wagons." (9) By 1851, members of the New York Knickerbockers, who headed west earlier, seeking their fortune, brought their version of the game to San Francisco and formed the San Francisco Knickerbockers Base Ball Club. (10)

CHAPTER 3

The National Pastime

a. The National Pastime/The National Association of Base Ball Players (NABBP)

b. Henry Chadwick

c. The Ballpark

d. The Great Rivalry - NYC vs. Brooklyn

e. Tammany Hall

f. College Base Ball

g. Women in Baseball

The National Pastime —

In December of 1856, a letter printed in the *New York Mercury* newspaper referred to base ball for the first time as the "national pasttime."(1) With the growing popularity of the sport in the northeast, the National Association of Base Ball Players (NABBP) was created a year later at a convention in New York City "for the purpose of discussing and deciding upon a code of laws which shall hereafter be recognized as authoritative in the game," as stated by Dean Sullivan in "Early Innings." (2) The convention also adopted the New York game's rules.

Daniel Lucius "Doc" Adams assumed the NABBP presidential duties, and the organization's prime purpose was the proliferation of the game. Economic opportunities were also a factor of the Association.

As expressed by George Kirsch the "New York" game was able to spread across the country due to "intercity competition, urban-rural interaction, newspaper publicity, New York City conventions, and feature events. It also provides a geography of early American baseball and suggests why the New York variety became the nation's leading sport." (3)

Henry Chadwick

Around the same time, a *New York Times* cricket journalist caught an intriguing glimpse of a ball game while witnessing a cricket match. British-born Henry Chadwick, a cricket journalist, knew a bit about the game but was now seeing the game of base ball in a new light. He immediately became enamored with this game played with a ball and a bat and how unique it was to the culture of his adoptive country. After witnessing a hard-fought contest between the Gotham and Eagle clubs of New York in the idyllic setting of Elysian Fields in Hoboken, Chadwick became a changed man. He enjoyed the style of the game, stating that "it suited the American temperament" while advocating the promotion of public health and exercise. He desired to make the game more "scientific" and more rugged, more "manly." (4) "Manly" was a charged word in the mid-nineteenth century, which helped to distinguish it from the earlier boys' game of "ball."

Chadwick became one of the earliest journalists to have a regular report on baseball as he drove steadily to rid the game of the on-going gambling and corruption. He was one of the first to use the now well-worn phrase "in the best interests of the game." Chadwick's articles in various publications such as the *New York Sunday Mercury* helped to push the "New York" game nationwide, including schedules and game results. And, in so doing, the town ball games of Boston and Philadelphia relented to the New York game's rules by 1860. The *Mercury* delivered everything from the season's schedule to game results with ball clubs, which was much appreciated by the fans. Chadwick also helped to develop the game's statistics, including the box score and the in-game scoring system as the editor of the highly respected publication, *Beadle's Dime Base-Ball Player.* In addition to other papers that he wrote for, such as the *Sporting Life* and the *Brooklyn Eagle,* Chadwick became the editor of the official guide of the National League, *Spalding's Official Base Ball Guide* in the early 1880s. (5) For all that he contributed to the game of base ball, Chadwick became the only journalist to be enshrined into the National Baseball Hall of Fame. Writers were later honored with the J.G. Taylor Spink Award, presented annually at the Hall of Fame for "meritorious contributions to baseball writing" and named after founder of *The Sporting News.* The award has been given annually since 1962.

The Ballpark

One of the wealthy entrepreneurs at this time was a gentleman by the name of William Cammeyer, who owned a plot of land in Brooklyn called "the Union Grounds" in 1862. He used his ground as the home field for teams from New York City, as well as from Brooklyn, which was not as much in demand. The coveted ground in New York City was always ripe for development, so Cammeyer saw potential revenue in

An early version of the 'clubhouse.'
Courtesy - Hall of Fame

the Union Grounds venue, which served as a skating rink in the winter. Cammeyer enclosed the field with a fence and built roofed seating with women spectators in mind. He also constructed clubhouses and charged a ten-cent admission fee. The "baseball park" was born. In *Ballpark: Baseball in the American City,* Paul Goldberger stated, "In the baseball park we can see how the country expressed a concept of community, and how we imbued the public realm with shared meaning." (6)

The Great Rivalry – "Great Baseball Match; All New York versus All

By the mid-19th century, Brooklyn was a hotbed of baseball, helping the New York area become the epicenter of the game. However, Brooklyn did not care too much about playing second-fiddle to New York City. As a result, in 1858, they challenged New York for bragging rights. A three-game match was played at the Fashion Course Racetrack on Long Island—near where Citi Field is located today—and admission charged. Attendance estimates during the three games ranged from 1,500 to 10,000. (7) The New York club came out on top by winning two out of

Brooklyn – Fashion Race Course, July 24, 1858
Courtesy - Library of Congress

the three games. Shortly after that, Philadelphia and Massachusetts abandoned their versions of Olympic ball and Town ball and conformed to the more popular New York game. This great rivalry continued through the next 100 years until it reached its peak in the 1950s. Many in Brooklyn were resistant to being incorporated into the New York City Charter in 1898. More on this will come later.

Tammany Hall

Tammany Hall was the most powerful and corrupt political organization in the history of New York City politics. William Magear "Boss" Tweed was elected to the United States House of Representatives in 1852 and the New York County Board of Supervisors in 1858, the year he became the head of the Democratic-controlled political machine known as "Tammany Hall." Tweed and Tammany Hall became synonymous, spawning an influential cadre of four corrupt politicians in 1858 known as the "Tweed Ring." The four members of the Tweed Ring were Oakey Hall, Peter Sweeney, Richard Connally and William Magear "Boss" Tweed. Not immune to corruption, New York's game became a prime target for fraud. The better amateur ballplayers on the team were paid "under the

Courtesy - Hall of Fame

table" from the City coffers either as street sweepers or through patronage jobs in the coroner's office. New York City thus owned the Mutuals with Tweed as a member of their board of directors. In 1865 the first public documentation of corruption in baseball came about when three New York Mutual ballplayers "fixed" a game against the Brooklyn Eckfords. (8)

It was also at this time that the city appropriated $250,000 to build a new courthouse. In 1871, the final tab came to $12,000,000, three-quarters of which lined the pockets of all the illicit contractors, an example of the corruption that the Tweed Ring wrought through Tammany Hall. Tammany Hall's power was increasing because they were capable of garnering votes from the poor at election time by doling out turkeys at Thanksgiving and cash at Christmas. The Tweed Ring appeared to be unstoppable. (9)

Ironically, the end of Tweed's reign came at the expense of a cartoon! In 1868, Thomas Nast, who many have claimed was "the father of

WHO STOLE THE PEOPLE'S MONEY ? — DO TELL . N.Y.TIMES.   'T WAS HIM.

The Tweed Ring consisting of corrupt New York City politicians,
led by William Magear "Boss" Tweed, that came together in 1858.
Courtesy - Library of Congress

the political cartoon," witnessed the corruption spewed by the Tweed Ring, and he decided to something about it. Nast also introduced the Republican "elephant" and popularized the Democratic "donkey" and the colorful Santa Claus (the donkey and Santa had earlier origins but became part of the American fabric by Nash's pen). In 1869, Nast had drawn a caricature of Tweed published in *Harper's Weekly* to great public appeal. The effect on Tweed did not go unnoticed, as claimed by author John Adler in his book, *Doomed by Cartoon*. Tweed stated, "Let's stop them damned pictures. I don't care much what the papers write about me---my constituents can't read, but damn it, they can see pictures." Ultimately, the law caught up with corruption wrought by Tweed and he was sent jail. After escaping jail, he took a circuitous route to Spain. There, he was recognized from one of Nast's cartoons and went back to the Ludlow Street jail, where he died of pneumonia in 1878, bringing this rendition of Tammany Hall to an end; only to be picked up by a more sophisticated and corruptive Tammany Hall. (10)

College Base Ball

While the Tweed Ring commanded New York, college baseball came on the scene in the northeast. A bitter rivalry between Williams College in western Massachusetts and Amherst College, more centrally located in the same state, began with the founding of Amherst in 1821. Zephaniah Swift Moore, the president of Williams, was dissatisfied with the distant location of Williams College in the northwestern corner of Massachusetts. He led a band of professors and students to join him in starting a college in the more centrally located area of Amherst. It began one of the greatest rivalries in college sports. In the groundbreaking game of 1859 in Pittsfield, Massachusetts, Amherst defeated Williams by the score of 73–32 under the Massachusetts game rules, which shortly after that gave way to the New York game's rules. (11) The first-ever nine-man team college baseball game under New York Rules played in New York on November 3, 1859, between the Rose Hill Baseball Club of Fordham, then called St. John's College, and St. Francis Xavier Preparatory, now known as Xavier High School. St. Johns beat St. Francis 33-11. (12)

As a sport, college baseball played second-fiddle to football and basketball since the late 19th century. The main reason for this occurrence is that baseball is a warm-weather sport, running from spring to fall. With college spring schedules ending in May or early June—and weather in many locales preventing schools from playing much before April—colleges were not able to play baseball for a substantial period, rendering the game a lesser sport. Another anomaly is that it is not inconceivable that a talented high school player would go directly to the professional minor leagues, whereas, in football and basketball, athletes often had at least a modicum of college experience before being accepted in the professional arena.

Nevertheless, college baseball has continued to grow in the past few decades, especially in warm-weather regions of the nation. Athletic directors, coaches, scouts, and recruiters began to see the potential appeal of the game. With increased revenue, baseball programs enabled their recruiters to pursue potential talent vigorously. More money poured in to upgrade the playing facilities as well as to support staff and sports promotions. As a result, more top-shelf players became attracted to college, and advancements in television programming and print media coverage began to blossom. ESPN networks have significantly increased television coverage of the NCAA playoffs and the College World Series.(13)

Women in Baseball

Women were not far behind with their introduction in college baseball. Vassar College was at the forefront of women playing organized baseball in 1866, spurring a rash of women's baseball in college. As reported by Daniel R. Epstein in *The Hardball Times,* "However, backlash from the public, press, and parents forced them to mostly shut down by the mid-1870s." (14)

The natural successor to college ball is professionalism, where women also gained a foothold. By the mid-1870s, women's competition emerged as two teams competed in Springfield, Illinois. And, it became the first known game of professional women ballplayers. Chester, Pennsylvania, was the home of the first African American professional women's ballplayers in 1883. (15)

The most significant attention that women professional ballplayers received came about in the 1890s when the "Bloomer Girls" went on barnstorming tours of the country. As stated in the *Science of Baseball Exploratorium*, "Amelia Bloomer designed and wore the loose-fitting, Turkish-style trousers that carried her name, and it made sports more practical for women athletes. In the 1890s, scores of 'Bloomer Girls' baseball teams blossomed all over the country. Eventually, many of them would abandon bloomers in favor of standard baseball uniforms." (16) A few major leaguers also donned the "Bloomer" outfit to play for the "Girls," notably the great Rogers Hornsby donned a wig as a teenager.

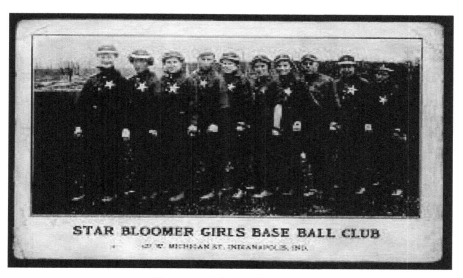

Courtesy - Library of Congress

CHAPTER 4

The Civil War Era

a. The Civil War/The Presidency and Base Ball
b. The New York City Draft Riots
c. Reconstruction Era/Negro Baseball
d. Segregation
e. Latino Baseball

The Civil War/The Presidency and Base Ball

This image depicts a 19th century baseball artifact marking the first time that a baseball image appeared on printed sheet music.
Courtesy - Library of Congress

n *Baseball in Blue and Gray*, George P. Kirsch said, "Baseball had clearly begun to acquire familiar connections with a love of country, freedom, virtue, morality, the work ethic, and other traditional American values." (1)

The Brooklyn Base Ball Club was baseball's first **champion in 1865**
Courtesy - Library of Congress

Courtesy - Hall of Fame

The Civil War/The Presidency of Base Ball

The national game. Three "outs" and one "run" by Currier & Ives: The American presidency began its long and steeped history with the national pastime starting with Abraham Lincoln, and the tradition has continued into the twenty-first century.

In 1860 a messenger from Washington, D.C., came to Abraham Lincoln's home in Springfield, Illinois, to inform him that a delegation would be arriving soon with a special announcement. To their dismay, they found "the great leader engaged in a game of Base Ball," according to Joel Zoss and John Bowman in *Diamonds in the Rough: The Untold History of Baseball*. Baseball mythmaker Albert Spalding later wrote that Lincoln advised the messenger, "Tell the gentlemen that I am aware of their coming; but they will have to wait until I make another base hit." (2)

The political cartoon, *The national game. Three "outs" and one "run,"* published in *Harper's Weekly* on September 15, 1860, satirizes Lincoln's victory in the 1860 election over Stephen Douglass, John Bell, and John C. Breckinridge as a base ball game.

When the Civil War broke out in 1861, thousands of northern baseball club members enlisted in the Union army while some volunteered for the Confederacy. The United States government permitted recreation at appropriate times as a necessary diversion to "preserve the soldier's health." Officers encouraged camp organized games to relieve the boredom. The games also helped motivate the men during training, foster group cohesion and loyalty, and improve recruits' physical fitness. (3)

While the Civil War ruptured the rapid growth that the game was experiencing, the war did help develop baseball in the South and West through captive Union soldiers in the Confederate prison camps. They, for the most part, played the New York game. The game also appealed to their Southern captors. As mentioned by George Kirsch, "Some observers viewed the introduction or revival of baseball in the border and southern states as a positive force in reuniting the nation after the Civil War." (4)

The New York City Draft Riots

President Abraham Lincoln issued the *Emancipation Proclamation* in September 1862. In the document, which was to go into effect on January 1, 1863, Lincoln called on the Union army to liberate all slaves in states still in rebellion as "an act of justice, warranted by the Constitution, upon military necessity." Slaves were declared to be "forever free." The proclamation exempted the border slave states that remained in the Union at the start of the Civil War and all or parts of three Confederate states controlled by the Union army. (5)

Many whites, particularly the Irish immigrants, then treated as second-class citizens, were furious over the fact that they were going to be on an equal status with African Americans. The government instituted a draft on all men between the ages of 20 and 45 through the Enrollment Act. However, a draftee could pay a $300 fee or obtain a substitute to fulfill his need to be involved in the war effort. The poor Irish working men could not afford to pay $300, and most of them could not obtain a substitute. The consignment fee precipitated the riots with the African Americans who had been taking low-end jobs from the Irish. During the ensuing riots, lasting from July 13-16, more than 100 died, and many more were injured before the New York State militia and volunteer troops were summoned from Gettysburg to quell the riots. (6)

Yet, base ball continued to spread outside of New York City. According to Zachary Brown in his *U.S. History Scene* article, Baseball, and the Civil War, "No sport looms larger in the public consciousness or historical memory than baseball. . . Once a regional sport confined to New York, the Civil War exposed baseball to a national audience and became a common interest that united both North and South." (8)

With base ball playing in parts of the south, especially in New Orleans, the exposure of the game to Confederate soldiers appeared in numerous illustrations.

Captain Otto Boetticher of the 68th New York Volunteers was a war prisoner. A commercial artist before the war, Boetticher was said to

Courtesy - Hall of Fame

Otto Boetticher, *Union Prisoners at Salisbury, N.C.*, Courtesy of Reynolds House
Museum of American Art, Winston Salem, North Carolina. (7)

have sketched the baseball scene pictured here on July 4, 1862. After he
was released a few months later, the sketch of this game was immortal-
ized in color when Currier & Ives purchased the rights to create this
lithograph. (9)

"The game broke down social barriers . . . improved camaraderie,
morale, and unity among the soldiers on both sides," Zachary Brown
wrote in his *U.S. History Scene*. "After the war, men enthusiastically
brought the New York variant of baseball home, making the sport a critical part of the reconstruction. Baseball emerged as a reflection of the
war's effect on the nation as a whole." (10)

The Thirteenth Amendment to the US Constitution, ratified in
1865, formally abolished slavery. While enabling equal rights for former
slaves, Lincoln opened the door for some African-Americans to enjoy
the right to vote. After Lincoln's assassination, President Andrew Johnson attempted to reverse much of the progress that his predecessor had
achieved. Apart from the requirement that they abolish slavery and reject
secession, he gave the new state governments the ability to manage their

affairs. African Americans strongly resisted these measures and seriously undermined Northern support for Johnson's policies.

Reconstruction Era/Negro Base Ball

The major problem of Reconstruction after the war was that the South took umbrage at Northerners who came to the South and the federal soldiers who stayed after the war to assist in maintaining order. The Fourteenth Amendment to the Constitution passed in 1868, granting citizenship and "equal protection of the laws" to all persons born or naturalized in the United States, which included former slaves. Toward the end of the Civil War, the first all-black baseball team, the Institute of Colored Youth, formed in Philadelphia. Octavius Catto was the fledgling team's captain and shortstop. Catto believed that a path to assimilation in the predominantly white society was through the burgeoning game. Catto, an educator and activist, along with Jacob White, formed the Knights of Pythias Base Ball Club in 1867. Part of the backlash was that black baseball teams were not granted entry into the National Association of Base Ball Players. (11)

Catto led a group of his students to the Pennsylvania statehouse after the Confederate invasion to Gettysburg in 1863 to answer the call to protect the state—only to be rebuffed. He went on to become a major in the Fifth Brigade, an all-black division of the National Guard. He also was a prominent figure in advancing the Fifteenth Amendment to the Constitution. The passage of the Fifteenth Amendment in 1870, granting equal rights to vote, gave rise to the formation of white supremacist groups, including the Ku Klux Klan (KKK). Sadly, on Election Day, 1871, white supremacist Frank Kelly, an ethnic Irishman, shot Octavius Catto in the back. He died from his wounds. (12) Catto was only thirty-two.

The deception of the recent Reconstruction era gains eventually led to the demise of equality through the Compromise of 1877. This informal agreement led to the withdrawal of all federal troops from the

Octavius Catto
Courtesy - Library of Congress

South, returning control to the individual states. Jim Crow laws were state and local laws re-enforced racial segregation in the Southern States. When enacted by white Democratic-dominated state legislatures, the rules lasted until 1965. (13)

Segregation

In 1885, baseball's first all-professional black base ball team, the New York Cuban Giants, began to play. (14) In 1887, the great ballplayer from the Chicago White Stockings, Adrian "Cap" Anson, a white supremacist, refused to play in a game against a Newark, New Jersey team that had two great African-American ballplayers, George Stovey, and, Moses "Fleetwood" Walker. (15) Six decades of segregation in Major League Baseball would follow before the color line broke.

Courtesy - Library of Congress

Latino Baseball

Baseball continued to spread during this period. Although the United States Navy was partially responsible for bringing the game of baseball to Cuba during an earlier deployment, it was Cuban-born Esteban Bellán, who participated in the original nine-man college game, that was responsible for bringing the New York game back to Cuba.

Bellán became the first Caribbean and the first Latin American to play professional baseball in the United States. Born in 1850 in Havana, Cuba, Bellán came to the United States at age thirteen. Seeking the benefits of a Jesuit education, he enrolled at St. John's Preparatory College (now Fordham University). (16) Bellán played for the Troy Haymakers and the New York Mutuals in the National Association of Base Ball Players. Upon returning to his home in Cuba, Bellán played and managed the first organized baseball game for the Havana team. (17)

The "Viva Baseball" exhibit at the National Baseball Hall of Fame in Cooperstown addresses the contributions of Latino baseball and focuses on Caribbean baseball, offering a deeper understanding of the importance of baseball in Latin American culture and the influence Latin players have on the game today. (Mitch Wojnarowicz/National Baseball Hall of Fame and Museum). (18)

CHAPTER 5

Professional Baseball and the Gilded Age

The Cincinnati Red Stockings - Professional Baseball

Toward the end of the 1860s, the game of baseball steadily improved and began to relinquish the image of being an amateur sport. In 1869, the Cincinnati Red Stockings then declared that all their players would be paid as true professionals. With the completion of the Transcontinental Railroad line in 1869, the Red Stockings went on a cross-country tour and won 69 games while not losing a single game. The impact of this achievement was the death knell to the amateur sport of base ball.

The National Association of Professional Baseball Players (NAPBBP)

With professionalism on the rise, two years later, in 1871, the first Major League of professional players, the National Association of Professional

Base Ball Players (NAPBBP), formed in Colliers Cafe at Broadway and 13th Street in New York City. (1) Not all the teams were in favor of going professional, and Tammany Hall still had a grip on the New York Mutual team. Nevertheless, the league opened in 1871 with a Boston Red Stockings team, who possessed most of the best talent in the game, winning four out of the five years (1872-1875) that the league was in existence the top rung. Unfortunately, the players who ran the teams did not possess much business understanding, and the League folded in 1875. In Charles Alexander's book, *Our Game-An American Baseball History*, he quoted Al Spalding's reason for the demise of the NAPBBP. "Professional baseball," Spaulding stated in 1875, "should be controlled by businessmen who would be in charge of conducting the details of managing men, administering discipline, arranging schedules and finding ways and means of financing a team." (2) No longer did the fraternally oriented professional people participate in the new league. Industrialization became evident to the ballplayers with the shortening of the working day as a result of robust mechanization enabling the workers to hone their baseball skills after the working day ended.

The Gilded Age

The age-old metaphor, "all that glitters is not gold," was without question applicable to this period. The Gilded Age, which lasted from the post-reconstruction Era around 1877 through the presidential election in 1896, brought an end to the Industrial Revolution from an agricultural society to an industrial one. (3) The Gilded Age also defined the extremes of political and economic culture. As illuminated by Esther Crain in her book, *The Gilded Age in New York 1870-1910,* "While much of the fractured nation was regrouping, New York was already on the rise, fueled by fortunes made from wartime financing and manufacturing."(4) Crain added, "New York in this era became a hub of invention and ingenuity, pioneering telephone service, artificial light, mass transit, ambulances and moving pictures." (5) As Crain moved toward societal issues, she wrote, "Social activism . . . labor rights, and children's welfare, suffrage, and independence of women set the stage for the city of the twentieth century to be one of the progressive ideals." (6)

A significant problem that persisted in the Gilded Age was Tammany Hall. Horror stories abound about the corruption and vice rampant in the infamous New York City Police Department from its top echelon heads to the lowly roundsmen. All were "on the take"! And, to the local merchants, there was a price to pay if you did not oblige the "protection" of the police department. The price might possibly be at the end of the policeman's nightstick. Rev. Charles Parkhurst, in 1892, was so incensed with the flagrant violations of the vice and corruption of the police department that he started preaching vitriolic anti-Tammany Hall sermons and exposing the vagaries of the New York Police Department (NYPD). By 1894, "legislative leaders in Albany announced a special senate committee, chaired by Sen. Clarence Lexow to investigate the NYPD from top to bottom," as stated by Daniel Czitrom in his book, *New York Exposed – The Gilded Age Police Scandal that Launched The Progressive Era."* (7)

Industrialization

America grew more prosperous due to the tremendous growth in industry and technology. Unfortunately, there was a cost to be paid by the working-class citizens. They were, in many cases, living under the most deplorable tenement conditions during the explosion of immigration that began in the 1870s. However, the end of the Gilded Age would eventually coincide with a significant political realignment in the watershed election of 1896.

Industrialization transformed American Society as it produced a new and wealthy class of industrialists and a prosperous middle class. (8) Industrialists such as John D. Rockefeller, J.P. Morgan, Andrew

The Tentacles of a Monopoly
Public Domain

Carnegie, and Cornelius Vanderbilt became tycoons (referred to as "Robber Barons)." They monopolized the industries of oil, steel, and transportation, and, at times, unscrupulously lending to the growth of blue-collar workers. The labor force that made industrialization consisted of millions of newly arrived immigrants and an even more significant number of migrants from rural areas further spurring urbanization. Diversification of America became the order of the day. (9)

Advertising

A new industry developed in 1869. Peck & Snyder, a sporting goods store in lower Manhattan, introduced the earliest version of the baseball card with a picture of the great 1869 Cincinnati Red Stockings Club. The fields of advertising and publishing greatly benefited from a new marketing idea as the cards encouraged buyers. Peck & Snyder went on to produce what are considered by some to be the world's first mass-produced baseball cards. (10)

Courtesy – The New York Times

In 1869, Peck & Snyder started printing trade cards, beginning with this photo of the undefeated Cincinnati Red Stockings. The 1911 cards distributed in cigarette packs, were the forerunners of modern sports trading cards.

John Montgomery Ward, great ballplayer
and organizer of the Players League
Courtesy - Library of Congress

Brooklyn Nationals star, Zack Wheat
Courtesy - Library of Congress

CHAPTER 6

The National League

a. **William Hulbert**
b. **The Reserve Clause**
c. **Albert Goodwill Spalding**
d. **The Beer and Whiskey League**
e. **Early Professional Baseball Clubs of New York**
f. **The Progressive Era**

William Hulbert

With the National Association of Professional Base Ball Players (NAPBBP) on the brink of destruction, William Hulbert, a Chicago coal merchant, came on the scene in 1874. Hulbert dearly wanted to wrest baseball's power base away from the established and corrupt eastern teams of the northeast. And, in doing so, it would help rebuild Chicago after the Great Fire of 1871 when more than half the city went up in flames.

Hulbert became president of the Chicago White Stockings in 1875. He sought out the best players by employing corrupt tactics of his own in the form of piracy. His first "capture" was one of the great ballplayers of the day, Al Spalding. Spalding grew up in Chicago but was playing for the mighty Boston Red Stockings. Hulbert convinced Spalding to come back home to Chicago, his first great coup. (1)

As the NAPBBP was sinking at that time, Hulbert corralled eight team owners, three of whom were new owners from the Midwest, to meet at the Grand Central Hotel in New York City. Strangely, Hulbert locked the door so that no one could leave or enter this crucial meeting, which gave birth to what became the National League.

The Reserve Clause

With the National League firmly in place, the team's owners began to experience a significant issue in contract restrictions. Up until this point, the players only needed to honor their contract for one year, thus, placing the owners in a quandary. In many cases, a player, after having a good season, was free to render his services to the higher or highest bidder for the following season, a term known as "revolving." The owners' response starting in 1980 was to agree that each team would be able to protect five players who were not allowed to be signed by other organizations. As defined in Baseball-Reference.com, "The reserve clause was a clause in player contracts that bound a player to a single team for a long period, even if the individual contracts he signed nominally covered only one season."(2) Hence, a player was locked in perpetuity to the team that he signed. So, no matter the success of the group, the players would not reap the rewards after a successful season(s). As hard as they may have tried to challenge this situation, the baseball owners were able to repel the players' advances for one hundred years. (See also chapter 5 Industrialization in this book).

Albert Goodwill Spalding

In 1876, Al Spalding joined the Chicago White Stockings as player-manager and as their ace pitcher to help inaugurate the new National

League, of which he became their shining star. He also brought along with him three of the best players from the Boston Red Stockings juggernaut team from that era. Spalding led his team to the pennant that first season.

After a stellar year pitching, which eventually helped him become elected into the Baseball Hall of Fame, Spalding became the first baseman in 1877. When he took his position, he wore a glove with no padding or fingers, risking ridicule from his teammates, for until then, baseball players had handled batted balls barehanded. Soon he designed a glove for protection from injury and began to market the concept in his family's sports shop in Chicago.

His idea caught on, and the company began to generate sales for his entrepreneurial endeavor. Spalding was a brilliant man who saw his ideas blossom into the most significant sports marketing business. He had an exceptional understanding of the business of baseball. His vision helped to develop the fledgling market of manufacturing sports equipment.

In 1876 Spalding and his brother J. Walter Spalding contributed $3,000, including an $800 loan from their mother, Harriet Irene Spalding, to open a business in the family's shop. Various types of gloves came into play. Fred Thayer introduced the catcher's mask in that same year. As a result of the booming success of the business, Spalding and his brother then opened the A.G. Spalding & Bros. Sporting Goods Company at 520 Fifth Avenue in New York City in 1885. For the 135 years since then, Spalding has been at the forefront of the sporting goods world. (3)

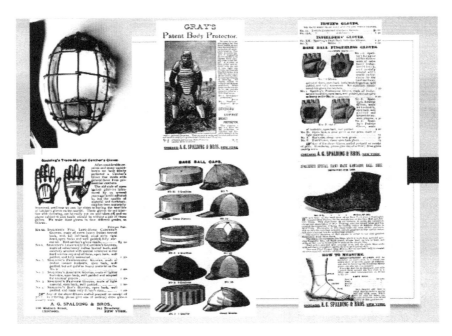

Courtesy - Library of Congress

Images of new equipment:

Courtesy - Library of Congress

The White Stockings sputtered in 1877, and Spaulding left the team to run his sporting goods firm. Spalding quickly tied his sporting goods firm to the future of the National League, earning the right to publish the official league book, which he titled, *Spalding's Official Baseball Guide*.

In addition, Spalding created the first official baseball of the National League. Later items to come from Spalding included bats, more gloves, hats, uniforms, golf clubs, footballs, basketballs, and various books. (4)

One of their most popular items, a pink rubber ball that was suited for the street games of stickball, stoop ball, king-queen, boxball, and off-the-curb—games played on paved city streets simulating a regular ball game—became eponymously known as a "Spalding."

Spalding's name was mentioned earlier for his contribution to the myth of Doubleday as base ball's founder. The story began as a disastrous barnstorming tour in England in 1889 when the British claimed that the game of baseball was nothing but a version of the English children's game of Rounders. However, upon his return home in a celebratory dinner at the famous Delmonico's Restaurant in New York, Spalding seized an opportunity to bring his myth about baseball's origins to the public. Two of the most popular celebrities in attendance were US Civil Services Commissioner, Theodore Roosevelt, and renowned author, Mark Twain. During an enthusiastic speech by the master of ceremonies, A.G. Mills, the crowd started chanting, "No Rounders." as a rebuke to the British in response to the aforementioned snub of our game of baseball. Mills would later chair a commission claiming that Abner Doubleday was the founder of the game in 1839, a myth later disputed by baseball historians. (5)

Al Spalding later established the Mills Commission in 1905 to assert that baseball had a pure American pedigree. Spalding, through the commission, further stated that the game had originated in Cooperstown, New York, in 1839. The only proof lay in the hands of Abner Graves, a character of dubious distinction, who presented (to) the commission, a ball found in an old trunk. Eventually, as new methods of baseball research grew, the Doubleday myth was debunked, but, as previously noted, it was not until after a plaque honoring Doubleday had been installed in the Baseball Hall of Fame in Cooperstown.

The Beer and Whiskey League

As the National League continued to grow, more cities sought to attract professional teams. Due to this popularity, there were attempts to form leagues to accommodate outlying towns and in some cases, in the larger cities where a team already existed. In the last three decades of the nineteenth century, nearly 900 baseball franchises opened. One of those upstart leagues was known as the American Association (AA) of Professional Baseball Clubs, also known as "The Beer and Whiskey League." In his book *The Beer and Whiskey League*, David Nemec stated, "The AA brazenly permitted the sale and consumption of intoxicating beverages at its games." Most of the team owners were beer barons. However, other differences between the two leagues included fees charged and playing days. The American Association charged half the price of the NL ticket, twenty-five cents as opposed to fifty cents. The AA also played baseball on Sundays, while the NL banned Sunday games. (6) Ultimately, the AA became the biggest threat to the National League from 1882-1891.

Early Professional Baseball Clubs of New York

The Metropolitan Baseball Club of New York became the first independent professional baseball club in New York City on September 15, 1880. Two weeks later, the Metropolitans opened the Polo Grounds as their home field, located between Fifth Avenue and Sixth Avenue from 110th Street to 112th Street. The New York Giants, (née the Gotham), played the first Major League game in the Polo Grounds on May 1, 1883. The Brooklyn Atlantics, formed in 1883, played their home games in Washington Park in the City of Brooklyn. After joining the American Association in 1884, they went on to win the AA Championship in 1889. After jumping over to the National League in 1890, the team won the NL Championship.

A watershed moment occurred in 1884 when the New York Metropolitans played in the first "World's Championship Series" against the Providence Grays in a best of five games. Unfortunately, they lost the Series in three games to the Providence Grays. The Grays' ace pitcher, Hoss Radburn, who won 60 games during the regular season, beat the Metropolitans in all three games. (7)

Baseball prospered at that time due to attractive advertising in colorful and informative publications. Superstars entered baseball drawing women to the game enticing the owners to initially promote "Ladies Days." A great ballplayer for the Chicago White Stockings, Michael Joseph "King" Kelly, who also was a flamboyant great looking guy, initially elevated to 'superstar' status. (8) Nevertheless, one major component was missing due to the ongoing segregation of negro ballplayers. Although civil rights had been granted to the people of color, most of the South did not want to hear of the newfound liberties that the Negroes were fully entitled to concerning the Fourteenth Amendment ratified in 1868.

One of the earliest all-black base ball clubs founded in 1866 was the Philadelphia Pythians Base Ball Club. As stated by Jared Wheeler in *Base Ball Founders*, "Their desire to emerge as a recognized amateur organization led to the first form of segregation in the game of base ball." (9) As a result, "black clubs sometimes also displayed the animosity and contentiousness exhibited by white organization," stated George B. Kirsch in *Baseball* in Blue and Gray

It was also around 1872 that English professor, Horace Wilson, introduced baseball to Japan at what is now known as Tokyo University. The game went on to become Japan's national pastime.

The Progressive Era.

Although the Progressive Era brought reform to government and business and increased political power for many citizens, its benefits were limited to white Americans; African Americans and other minorities continued to experience discrimination and marginalization during this era, as stated in *lumen learning*. (11) The gulf between the upper and lower classes was exposed by muckraking journalist Jacob Riis when he explored the harsh realities of tenement life in his book *How the Other Half Lives*. His work precipitated the New York State legislature to examine and deal with the decrepit and overcrowding of the tenement housing problems. (12)

The transformation in American society coincided with the rise of Progressivism in the 1890s into the early 1900s. Peter Panacy in *Bleacher Report*, "Major League Baseball Finds Its Roots in Progressive America" wrote:

> **"The radical shift in American society that accompanied the rise of Progressivism in the late 19th and early 20th centuries influenced, and arguably was influenced by, the growing popularization of baseball. Whether American citizens realized it or not, the sport showcased aspects of their daily lives. With the drastic changes brought by the Progressive Era, baseball too saw its own changes." (13)**

The changes enhanced the growth and popularity of the game as new rules were inserted into the game, similar to the new regulations brought about by the modern Progressive politicians. The ideology of Progressivism came at a time when the Gilded Age and Tammany Hall was still running rampant with corruption. Baseball had not been exempt from this situation. The teams' owners acted more like autocrats since professional baseball had come on the scene in the early 1870s. As professionalism continued to grow through the 1880s, baseball became more of a model for corporate America to examine as the game required both individualism and teamwork. Baseball historian Steven Gelber stated, "Baseball also represented the relationship of urban life, business organization, and the values that underlay them. The growth of baseball as a professional sport significantly impacted how America viewed the game and how baseball would influence Americans during the Progressive Era." (14)

During this time, three other leagues formed to oppose the Reserve Clause mentioned earlier. In 1884, the Union Association; In 1889, the Players League attempted to challenge the monopolistic National League and the aforementioned American Association. (15) Financial woes ended the Union Association after the 1884 season. Later, the Players League formed in 1890, headed by John Montgomery Ward, under the premise of circumventing the Reserve Clause, folded in January of 1891 due to financial constraints. (16) It turns out that Ward and these short-lived leagues were prescient in knowing that opposition to the reserve clause was a harbinger of things to come, but it took 75 years before Marvin Miller came on the scene to help abolish this clause.

At the end of 1891, the American Association went under, and the National League once again monopolized league baseball. The NL extended the league from eight to twelve teams, thus spreading the better talent thin. In 1893, a new Minor League, the Western League (WL), brought to the game a more respectful decorum that had not existed in the National League. The WL promoted a cleaner brand of baseball, challenging the unruly tactics employed by the National League.

Author Melvin Adelman stated, "Historians are in agreement that the rise of sport in America occurred in the last three decades of the nineteenth century and that urbanization/industrialization was the major impetus." (17)

PART TWO

CHAPTER 7

The American League

a. Tammany Hall Redux
b. The Lexow Committee
c. Andrew Freedman
d. Ban Johnson/ John McGraw
e. The American League/New York City
f. The World Series

Tammany Hall Redux

By the early 1890s, Tammany Hall still held its grip on the political arena in New York City. The New York Police Department (NYPD) was scandalous. Even the crash of the stock market in 1893 was of little consequence to their machine. However, as mentioned in Chapter Five, Reverend Charles Parkhurst, a leader in the temperance movement and a longtime social reformer, enlightened his congregation to the vices and vicissitudes of Tammany through his sermons. (1) Parkhurst's observations persuaded Clarence Lexow of the State Legislature to initiate an inquiry into the city's corruption in 1894 after a personal undercover three-week tour of the "tenderloin" (an area on the west side of New York City where vice and corruption flourished). (2)

The Lexow Committee

The Lexow Committee (1894 - 1895) was the New York State Senate investigation of Tammany's ties to New York's rampant corruption. This commission was precipitated by Parkhurst's crusade against vice and crime in
New York City. "They are a lying, perjured, rum-soaked and libidinous lot,"
stated Parkhurst. The committee produced damning evidence that the police
fostered vice and corruption and were responsible for rigged elections. (3)
The allegations stated that the main suspect of this corruption was none
other than the Police Commissioner, William "Big Bill" Devery. The Lexow
Committee findings severely wounded Tammany Hall in the 1894 municipal election, loosening a good bit of control on the political scene. Many said
that Devery was the most corrupt police commissioner in the history of the
City of New York's politics whose motto was "see, hear and say nothing; eat,
drink and pay nothing." When reformer Theodore Roosevelt became the
New York City police commissioner in 1895, he placed Devery squarely in
his crosshairs. Roosevelt even had to fight members of his party corrupted
by the Tammany faction. In 1897, Roosevelt vacated his position to become
Assistant Secretary of the United States Navy. Then, in 1899, the investigation by the Mazet Commission fired another broadside at Tammany Hall,
further decimating its corrupt grip on politics. (4) Ultimately, in January
of 1902, Devery was fired by Seth Low, the new mayor of New York City,
which would prove to be, 'a blessing in disguise.'

Andrew Freedman

In 1895, Andrew Freedman had bought into the New York Giants.
Freedman was also a close friend and business partner of then Tammany
boss Richard Croker. As stated by Frank Graham in *The New York Giants:
An Informal History of a Great Baseball Club*, "For eight years, Freedman
ruled the Giants and almost completely wrecked them. Had he not been
restrained, he would have wrecked the league as well." (5) Furthermore,
Freedman irritated the other team owners when he attempted to syndicate

what he called the "National League Trust." The common stock would be used in payment for the eight clubs with New York to receive 30%, and the rest of the league to receive between 12% and 6% for each. (6)

Al Spalding, who was an integral part of professional baseball's early development, could not stand by and watch this travesty unfold from the sidelines. Using an improperly held election in the spring of 1902, Spalding bluffed Freedman into thinking that his bold attempt to refashion baseball to fit his own needs had split the league-wide open and that further measures on his part were bound to fail. As a result, Freedman promised to resign as soon as he could find a suitable buyer for the Giants. (7)

Ban Johnson/John McGraw

With the National League as the only major game in town, the Minor Western League, with Ban Johnson at its helm, took great strides in advancing their game with a cleaner brand of baseball. Concluding the 1890s, the National League had to shed a few of their weaker teams from their over-weighted 12-team league. The Western League absorbed four teams and declared Major League status in 1900. In 1901, Johnson renamed the Western League the American League. He began to raid the National League for some of their best ballplayers, which helped Johnson gain parity with the well-established National League.

The new league consisted of eight teams: Baltimore, Boston, Chicago, Cleveland, Detroit, Milwaukee, Philadelphia, and Washington. What was missing, Johnson felt, was a New York entry. He knew that he could not sustain a challenge to the National League without New York. However, every time that he approached the city to acquire a parcel of land to turn into a ballpark, an unexpected obstacle arose. With the help of Richard Croker, Freedman's close associate on the Real Estate Board of New York City, they repelled every attempt on Johnson's part to gain the desperately needed land.

Johnson also had another problem—Baltimore Orioles' part-owner, manager, and ballplayer, John McGraw. McGraw was from Tuxedo, NY, and he fervently desired to manage the New York entry in the American League. However, the foul mouthing and dirty tactics that McGraw used during games and his at times ferocious umpire baiting, were not favored by Ban Johnson. McGraw's continuous run-ins with Johnson eventually wound up with McGraw suspended in July of 1902. McGraw then allied with Andrew Freedman, who was still keeping any competition with his Giants out of New York City. McGraw and Freedman crafted a deal whereby McGraw would release most of his best Oriole ballplayers to Freedman and the Giants when he jumped away from the American League. McGraw went to the Giants in the National League as their player-manager and co-owner. (8) His actions sorely depleted the Baltimore team, and Ban Johnson had to reach out to other American League teams to refill the roster.

Christy Matthewson
Courtesy - Hall of Fame

After the season was over, the Orioles became defunct, thus opening the door for a new entry, eventually to be named "The Greater American League Baseball Club of New York."

Christy Mathewson-HOF was the New York Giants star pitcher in the early decades of the 20th century, and a Bucknell graduate. Quiet, soft-spoken, Mathewson, was a beacon of light that led McGraw's Giants to their great success during the "Deadball" era. Matty, as he was known, volunteered his services to the World War I effort in 1918.

Unfortunately, he inhaled mustard gas during a training exercise, which culminated in tuberculosis that took his life in 1925. (9)

The American League and New York City

Two seasons had gone by, and still there was no land in New York for an American League Ballpark. However, with Tammany weakened further as a result of the Mazet Commission's latest investigation in 1899, another powerful faction in Tammany Hall gained strength. By the end of 1902, a sportswriter named Joe Vila introduced Johnson to two Tammanyites—the aforementioned New York City police chief Bill Devery and "poolroom king" Frank Farrell. With the background support from anti-Tammany leader "Big Tim" Sullivan, they were able to pick up the vacated Baltimore charter for the Greater American League Baseball Club of New York on March 11, 1903. (9) Devery and Farrell were able to locate a rocky site for a ballpark for Johnson on Broadway between 165th Street and 168th Street. The New York franchise now became a member of the American League. The team played in a hastily constructed, all-wood park at 168th Street and Broadway. Because the site is one of the highest spots in Manhattan, the club became known as the "Highlanders" and their home field as "Hilltop Park." (10)

However, the term Highlanders did not sit well with the neighborhood's Irish residents as it was the name of a Scottish Regiment in the Revolutionary War. Additionally, the limitations of the linotype, since its invention in 1886, also made the team's long name too cumbersome for the press to fit in the narrow columns of the tabloids. The term "Yankees" appeared in the media after spring training in 1903 when the team was leaving the South to prepare for opening day. The main headline in the sports section that day was "Yankees" Come North. They adopted the now world-renowned "NY" logo on their uniform in 1909. (11) Both names, Highlanders and Yankees, were intermittently used until 1912, when the team moved to the New York Giants' Polo Grounds for the 1913 season. At that time, they became known exclusively as the New York Yankees.

The World Series

The two top teams in baseball in 1903, the National League's New York Giants and the Boston Americans squared off for baseball supremacy in the best five out of nine series to determine the "world's champion." Enter the "fall classic," the first Major League Baseball World Series played in 1903 between the Pittsburgh Pirates and the Boston Americans. The Boston team prevailed. However, in 1904 McGraw, perhaps with a little residual enmity for Ban Johnson's American League (AL), refused to play the American League champion team. McGraw claimed that the fledgling AL was an inferior league, thus taking a parting shot at Johnson as AL president. However, McGraw did resume World Series play in 1905 as his NL Champion Giants defeated the AL Champion Philadelphia A's. (12)

A few years later, Albert Von Tilzer (1878–1956) and Jack Norworth (1879–1959) wrote, "Take Me Out to the Ball Game." New York: New York Music Co., 1908.

As the story goes, in 1908, singer and songwriter Jack Norworth was traveling on a New York City subway headed to perform at a theater with nothing prepared. He saw a sign that said, "Baseball Today-Polo Grounds" which inspired him to jot down his thoughts, "Katie Casey was baseball mad, had the fever and had it bad. When her beau asked if she would like to see a show, Katie said, "No," but what you can do is . . .

Courtesy - Music Division, Library of Congress

"Take me out to the ball game,
Take me out with the crowd.
Buy me some peanuts and crackerjack,
I don't care if I never get back,
Let me root, root, root for the home team,
If they don't win, it's a shame.
For it's one, two, three strikes, you're out,
At the old ball game." (13)

The song became so popular that it is now sung in nearly every ballpark during the "seventh inning stretch." It has been ranked in survey polls as one of the top ten songs of the twentieth century and is behind only to "Happy Birthday" and "The Star Spangled Banner" as the most easily recognized songs in America.

Stage star Georgia Caine, shown seated with her dog, leads a carload of Pittsburgh and New York pennant-wielding fans from the Lyric Theatre to a game in July 1909 aboard a Studebaker touring car.

Courtesy - Library of Congress

CHAPTER 8

A New Regime

a. Jacob Ruppert
b. Boston Red Sox and Harry Frazee
c. The Star-Spangled Banner
d. The Deal of the Century
e. The Black Sox Scandal

Jacob Ruppert

Jacob Ruppert, Sr. came to the US from Bavaria, Germany, and opened a brewery on 94th Street and 5th Avenue in 1867. When son Jacob Ruppert, Jr. took over the running of the Knickerbocker Beer brewery, he needed a little boost to grab the top spot in the beer market. (1) Jacob Ruppert Jr. joined Tammany Hall in 1899, and his membership helped put him where he wanted to be—on top of the beer world. Knickerbocker beer was poured in every Tammany Hall bar and speakeasy in the City, and soon after that, it reached the top of the market. Tammany recognized Ruppert's rise by giving him a spot on the Finance Committee, ironically alongside Andrew Freedman, the man reviled by the National

League team owners. Ruppert was then tapped by "boss" Croker to run for Congress to cultivate the much needed and rising German vote. Ruppert followed the Tammany line while serving four terms from 1899 to 1907. (2)

Upon leaving Congress in 1907, Ruppert immersed himself in his brewery business. Stout added, "He owned yachts, raced horses, bred dogs, and collected exotic animals, jade, porcelain, and first editions, and, as a lifelong bachelor, mistresses." (3) He always had an interest in owning a baseball team, preferably the New York Giants. The Giants' manager, John McGraw, introduced Ruppert to his friend, civil engineer Captain Tillinghast L'Hommedieu Huston, who made his fortune in the Spanish American war. However, the Giants would not be the team that Ruppert and Huston would acquire.

After an exciting season in 1904 when the Boston Pilgrims and the New York Highlanders went to the end of the season vying for first-place honors, the team was pretty much a non-entity in the future pennant races. The two owners, Devery and Farrell, who were not baseball connoisseurs and were unable to procure the right talent, lasted until 1914 when they had to sell the team, partly due to personality conflicts, but mostly because of financial constraints. American League president Ban Johnson did not want to see his coveted New York franchise go under, so he sought out parties financially stable enough to discuss the sale of the franchise.

On January 14, 1915, *The New York Times* posted that Ruppert and Huston jointly paid $450,000 (of which Ruppert paid his half with a check and Huston paid his half in $1,000 bills) to Devery and Farrell. This marked the beginning of the New York Yankees' iconic history. American League president Ban Johnson was instrumental in some top-grade talent to ensure that New York was a viable entry. The new owners also looked for additional talent to make the Yankees more competitive as they needed the caliber of their Yankee team worthy of the status of New York City.

Boston Red Sox and Harry Frazee

The Boston Red Sox, meanwhile, won three out of the next four World Series—1915, 1916, and 1918. One of the stars contributing to this success was a talented 20-year-old pitcher named George Herman "Babe" Ruth. Babe had lived in St. Mary's Industrial Home for Boys since 1907, as his parents were not able to give him the proper care in their home. It was here that Brother Matthias saw Babe's natural talent and helped him develop into an exceptional young athlete.

Babe Ruth's playing career started in the Baltimore farm system in 1914. The Red Sox then purchased his contract at the end of 1914. The Babe went on to become one of the greatest pitchers in the game through the end of the decade. Many have said that if the Babe had not become the premier slugger of all time, he was still likely to become a Hall of Famer as a pitcher with a sparkling .671 winning percentage.

The problem was that Babe knew he was a star in the clubhouse, and he was always looking for special treatment. Besides being one of the largest players in the league, he was cantankerous, obnoxious at times, and a detriment to his teammates through his behavior. Babe's attitude may be one of the reasons that the Red Sox traded the great pitcher Carl Mays to the Yankees in a disputed deal that went to court. The judge ruled in favor of the Yankees. Babe Ruth, released from the discipline of St. Mary's, now looked at life through a completely different lens. His unbounded appetite for life, especially for nightlife, got him into frequent trouble.

The Star-Spangled Banner

In the 1918 World Series, a precedent was set that has continued to the present time. The Boston Red Sox and the Chicago Cubs opened the World Series to the strains of the "Star-Spangled Banner." Its history dates back to 1814 when Francis Scott Key published the lyrics. It became a tradition at baseball games to open the events with this song. Other sports followed suit. In 1931, the "Star-Spangled Banner" became the National Anthem. (4)

This year also brought an influenza pandemic with a highly contagious strain that spread across the United States and the world. The deadly disease known as the Spanish Flu killed an estimated 675,000 Americans, which has drawn much attention lately due to the upsurge in the Coronavirus (COVID-19) pandemic, which until this date killed over 520,000 Americans. Bill Francis of the Hall of Fame stated:

Baseball was not immune. The 'Spanish flu' lasted just fifteen months but killed, according to best estimates today, between 50 million and 100 million worldwide. It infected an estimated 500 million people around the world, about a third of the planet's total population. Sportswriters, a handful of minor and major league ballplayers, and the popular Major League umpire, Silk O'Loughlin, all succumbed to the insidious disease. (5)

The Deal of the Century

Red Sox owner Harry Frazee was deeply concerned about Babe Ruth. Was the Babe too disrupting in the clubhouse? Would he renege on his contract of $10,000 per year over three years, wanting Frazee to double it? Frazee was worried that the Babe might skip the team altogether, as he had done in the past, leaving Harry Frazee (Big Harry) holding the bag with nothing to show for it. True, Ruth was the greatest ballplayer at the time, and the fans understandably did not want to see him go, but at what price would Frazee keep him? The feeling appeared mixed in the Boston press.

Frazee was a New Yorker at heart. His great-grandson, Max Frazee, whose family grew up in New York City, stated that Harry felt "the best thing about Boston was the train ride back to New York." A successful entrepreneur and theatrical producer on Broadway, Harry Frazee was highly respected in New York. He had established a friendship with Yankees' owners Ruppert and Huston through a theater group called the Lambs Society.

At one social meeting, the Red Sox owner opened a dialogue on Babe Ruth's future. Besides being a nuisance in the clubhouse, Ruth, coming off a record-breaking year by hitting 29 home runs, more than any other player in baseball's history, demanded his $10,000 per annum salary be doubled for three years as Frazee feared. Frazee thought the Red Sox had already lost perhaps the best player in the game, Tris Speaker, in 1915, but the club wound up winning two World Series after that in 1916 and 1918. It was too much for the business sense of Harry Frazee to give into Ruth's demands.

While Ruth was vacationing in Hollywood, California, in December 1919, threatening to take on acting or a boxing career, Frazee contemplated what the future might entail with and without the Babe. He did not have to look too far for buyers. His friends Ruppert and Huston had the resources necessary to purchase such an essential asset for their Yankees.

Much to the dismay of the Boston fans, Frazee chose to sell Babe Ruth's contract. Frazee struck a deal with the New York Yankees, giving up the Babe for $100,000 and a $350,000 loan with Fenway Park as collateral. The "Deal of the Century," as many called it, became history on Dec. 26, 1919, but it was not announced publicly until January 3, 1920, as they waited for Babe Ruth's return to New York from his vacation in Hollywood. (6)

In opposition to the general public's reaction, Boston sportswriter Paul Shannon stated that

Ruth has hurt morale considerably . . . if Ruth makes good on his threat and retires from the game, he will be sadly missed. However, even as a big figure as Ruth is, the public would soon forget all about him [because] a contract is a contract. Right is right in Baseball as anything else. (7)

In a telephone interview with Harry's great-grandson, Max Frazee, Max said, "Big Harry" or "Handsome Harry" is what I have known of him all my life. Most of the time, when others speak of him, it concerns which side of 'The Curse of the Bambino' does one believe. Max went on to say that there was "not much more to the story except for the fans' hurt feelings."

Max said, "Harry has had this following him ever since he sent Ruth to the Yankees from Boston. After many years have passed, the myth 'The Curse of the Bambino' was created for the entertainment of others. It seems that many people will want to hear this story because it is more interesting than the truth. I have read through all of them and usually have a good laugh at all the theories concerning Harry."

"Harry was his own man with interests in theater, boxing, and real estate. His successes were not so much in baseball but on Broadway. He produced about 60 Broadway plays; some played worldwide. Harry was an entrepreneur. He built the Longacre Theatre in New York City in 1912-13, he purchased the Harris Theatre in 1920, and also acquired the Lyric Theatre in New York City and the Arlington Theatre in Boston. In 1907, he built the Cort Theatre in Chicago. Harry was 27 years old at that time. I could go on and on, but I find that it will be impossible to stop the lies and presumptions about my great grandfather." (8) The myth or speculations Max Frazee referred to centered around Big Harry selling Ruth's contract because he needed money to support his theater business.

The Black Sox Scandal

Legend has it that the 1919 Chicago White Sox ballplayers were unhappy with their paychecks, making this situation rife for exploitation. The gambling community, always looking for opportunities of this nature, heard of the ballplayers' plight. All this made for the prime-time theater. Author David Pietrusza in his book *Rothstein* stated, "The Black Sox Scandal is not just a riddle wrapped in an enigma inside a mystery. It is a labyrinth of fixes, double-crosses, cover-ups, and con so big, so audacious, it nearly ruined professional baseball." (9) The man referenced as pulling all the strings was underworld kingpin, Arnold Rothstein.

Eight disgruntled players of the heavily favored Chicago White Sox conspired to let the underdog Cincinnati Reds win the Series in return for the promise of $5,000, which was around the average salary for each of the White Sox players for 1919. The Reds won the World Series five games to three. Ultimately, not one of the involved players received their full share of their promised money. After the plot was exposed with the eight players indicted, the new Commissioner of Baseball, Judge Kennesaw Mountain Landis (his birthright name), came on to protect the game's integrity. This "Black Sox" scandal thus became a huge black eye for the national pastime. (10) It is fair to say that although the "Black Sox Scandal" was one of the greatest, if not THE greatest travesty of baseball, it was not the first of its kind.

CHAPTER 9

The Roaring Twenties

The Babe Comes to Town

The Progressive Era of social and political reform focused on the progress toward a better society ended after World War I. On the heels of the Spanish flu in 1918, the Black Sox scandal of 1919, ratification of the Eighteenth Amendment prohibiting the sale, manufacture, and transportation of alcoholic beverages (the Prohibition Era), and the passage of the Nineteenth Amendment enabling women the right to vote, the stage was set for a renaissance. Baseball in New York promised to play a big part.

As good fortune would have it, the Black Sox case did not adjudicate until late in 1920. This was a blessing in disguise as baseball received a tremendous boost from the performance of the new Yankee in town, Babe

Ruth. The Babe hit 54 home runs in his first year with New York. Keep in mind that no other team in the American League totaled that no more than 50 home runs. Ruth's feat eclipsed by 25 runs the record of 29 home runs he hit the prior year. Amazing!

The Brooklyn Dodgers, (at that time known as the Brooklyn Robins), bystanders in the sports headlines due to the success of the New York Giants in the National League, finally made it to post-season play in 1920 for the first time in three decades, only to lose to the Cleveland Indians. In the next four years, the Giants won four pennants while the Yankees won three pennants. It took two more decades for the Dodgers to climb back into contention.

New rules passed that increased the action in the game dramatically. In 1920 the baseball owners decided that the low scoring games were very dull. Scores were low because only one ball was used for the entire game, rendering it dead by the late innings. Thus, these first two decades became known as the "dead ball" era. Baseball's hierarchy decided that the baseballs would be changed frequently during the game, and the balls would be more tightly wound by machine to enhance the baseball's liveliness.

Furthermore, pitchers were not allowed to put any foreign substances on the baseball that would alter the ball's trajectory, thus helping the batter get a clearer vision of the straighter trajectory of the ball. The Spalding Sporting Goods Company benefited greatly by these changes in the rules since the rules created increased sales of the game's equipment. It became a different ballgame as soon as these rules went into effect. As a result of this change, there came an offensive explosion that excited the fans. The home run became the singular most exciting moment of the game, bringing the fans to their feet.

The nation dealt with the Spanish Flu, Prohibition, and the Black Sox Scandal in their national pastime. But it was Babe Ruth and his home runs who brought life to the game. Ruth was on his way to becoming the legend still talked about today. During this period, Babe Ruth led the Yankees to their first pennants and World Series victories while leading the band into the Roaring 20s as they began their march to winning a phenomenal 27 World Series. The closest team to that mark is the St. Louis Cardinals with eleven World Series championships. The 1920s was the decade when baseball stamped its identity indelibly on American popular culture, and Yankee Stadium, a.k.a. "The House that Ruth Built" was the place where it all happened. The Roaring 20s, indeed!

Radio and Automobiles

While the attendance at the games continued to rise as a result of the increase in offense, interest in the game spread to more extensive areas through the advent of radio broadcasts and the popularity of the automobile. Baseball went on air for the first time when Pittsburgh radio station KDKA broadcasted a game between the Pirates and the Philadelphia Phillies on August 5, 1921, with announcer Harold Arlin. (1) Although automobiles started to come on the scene around the turn of the century, it wasn't until Henry Ford built a massive automotive complex in Dearborn, Michigan in the early'20s that there was a surge in the industry's growth. (2)

Yankee Stadium

Opening Day, Yankee Stadium April 18, 1923
Courtesy – Hall of Fame

As a result of the Yankees' success by winning the American League pennants in 1921 and 1922, Jacob Ruppert, who longed for his own ballpark, finally saw his dream come into fruition. On a ten-acre plot of land on the south side of 161st Street and River Avenue in the Bronx, NY, less than a mile from the Polo Grounds, Yankee Stadium was built for $2.4 million, ultimately becoming not only the green cathedral to baseball but also the mecca for many outdoor events in our country.

The first papal mass in the Western Hemisphere was celebrated at the Stadium on October 4, 1965, by Pope Paul Vl. Two more papal masses followed in 1979 and 2008. Soccer got a toe-hold in the United States with the great Brazilian star, Pele, in 1976. Thirty professional championship fights at Yankee Stadium as well as circuses, rodeos, motorcycle racing, women's exhibition baseball, college, and professional football, Jehovah's Witnesses events, the Billy Graham Crusade programs and other interdenominational faith healings, Nelson Mandela, Negro Baseball from 1936-1947, the memorial following the attack on the World Trade Center on September 11, 2001, the greatest professional football game with the New York Giants and the Baltimore Colts for the 1958 National Football League Championship, and two outdoor NHL games have all been a part of the Yankee Stadium mosaic. President George W. Bush made the ceremonial first pitch in Game 3 of the dramatic 2001 World Series. The only drawback to this stadium was the lack of parking availability as ballparks built during the early rise of the automobile did not have parking spaces on the agenda.

The Farm System

The excitement of increased fan attendance during the 1920s materialized both socially and financially. The owners saw the advantages of this surge of interest in the game and introduced new methods to improve their product. One of the great innovators of baseball during this time was St. Louis Cardinals General Manager, Branch Rickey. (3) Rickey introduced a system whereby his scouts scoured designated areas for new and better talent. He then purchased teams at rock bottom prices to secure the more talented players. As the beginning of the "farm system" took hold, other clubs witnessed the fruits of this system and followed suit. (4)

The Negro Leagues

The Negro National League also saw its beginning in 1920 with the "father of black baseball," Rube Foster, as its principal architect. In the 1920s, the Negro League talent appeared at least on a level equal to their white brethren. According to the noted authority on Negro baseball, John B. Holway in *The Complete Book of Baseball's Negro Leagues: The Other Half of Baseball History,* "The Negro League ballplayers playing against teams with white Major Leaguers won 268 games vs. 168 wins for the white Major Leaguers." (5) In his book *Josh and Satch,* on two of the greatest ballplayers, Josh Gibson and Satchel Paige, Holway wrote, "On April 28, 1930, the first professional night games had taken place. The Kansas City Monarchs and the Independence, Kansas, team each turned on their separate lighting systems 100 miles apart. (In 1927, two Massachusetts teams, Salem and Lynn, had played a night game in Lynn; both were members of the New England League, but it is not clear whether this was an official game.) At any rate, the experiments would save both black baseball and white minor leagues during the long decade of hard times ahead." It was of great importance to the Negro Leagues, especially during the depression when renting fields was much too expensive. (6) (7)

CHAPTER 10

The Depression Era

a. The Depression
b. The Called Shot
c. The All-Star Game
d. Night Baseball/Radio
e. Ethnicity
f. The Hall of Fame
g. Lou Gehrig

The Depression

The Depression Era that followed the stock market crash of 1929 witnessed the loss of one-third of the job market. According to *The Official Encyclopedia of Major League Baseball, Total Baseball, Sixth Edition,* attendance at baseball games fell 40 percent from 1930 to 1933. It did not return to pre-Depression attendance until after World War ll. While baseball was affected by the crash and the ensuing Depression, it stayed strong. (1) President Herbert Hoover, at the time, stated, "Next to religion, baseball has furnished a greater impact on American life than any other institution."

The federal government decided that it would impose a 10 percent amusement tax on ticket prices in 1932 and 1933. Baseball club owners shortened the rosters and made pay cuts to help defray the loss of revenue coming through the turnstiles. The only two teams to wind up in the black in 1932 were the two World Series contenders, the Chicago Cubs and the New York Yankees.

During the Depression, the corporate structure understandably continually sought new avenues to claim fading consumer dollars. Major League Baseball responded by scheduling night games in 1935, an innovation far more appealing in the minor leagues than in the majors, and by broadcasting games on the radio. All organized baseball clubs recognized the wisdom of hiring press agents and publicity directors to curry favor with sportswriters and to bolster attendance. Owners realized that their stadia were vacant much of the time. With the Negro Leagues making great strides during the 1920s, New York Yankees owner, Jacob Ruppert, seeing an opportunity for additional revenue, began renting Yankee Stadium to the Negro Leagues from 1936 through 1947. Yankee Stadium became home to the Black Yankees Baseball Team.

The Called Shot

One of the greatest legendary moments in the annals of sports history came in Game 3 of the 1932 World Series at Wrigley Field in Chicago. The story centered around the well-liked former Yankees shortstop, Mark Koenig, who went to the Chicago Cubs in August 1932 and was instrumental in the Cubs' pennant run. When the Yankees heard that Koenig was only going to receive a half-share of the World Series paycheck, they openly taunted the Cubs and their fans.

As Babe Ruth stepped up to the plate in the third inning with two men on base, Cubs pitcher Charlie Root threw a called strike. This moment was the beginning of a never-ending debate. The Babe pointed toward Root that this was only one strike. The next pitch was strike two. The same scenario followed with the Babe pointing again that there were now two strikes as he jawed with the Cubs dugout, gesticulating his response to the players' torments, waving his arms at their bench. The fans went wild at this point. It may have seemed that the Babe was pointing to the flagpole in centerfield, indicating where the next pitch was going to wind up. Of all eyewitnesses to the scene, half-believed the pointing version to centerfield and half did not. (2)

This writer had the good fortune of watching amateur photographer, Bill Candaele's version, as his 16mm camera caught the action of the Babe's home run from behind home plate. It appeared to me that Babe Ruth did not point to a specific spot. However, it was quite amazing watching the Babe rounding the bases and provoking the Cubs en route to the Yankees' dugout. The Cubs pitcher, Charlie Root, who didn't think that he pointed, said that "if he thought that the Babe was pointing at him, the next pitch that he threw would be in his ear." Cubs catcher Gabby Hartnett also believed that the Babe was not trying to show anybody up with the pointing. After the game, when asked by a reporter if he pointed, Babe said, "No, I didn't point." However, later on, with all the coverage that this event had generated, Babe, ever the showman, seeing that this moment had taken on a life of its own said, "Well, after I had two strikes, I pointed to the bleachers in centerfield." The Yankees won the game and went on to beat the Cubs in Game 4 to sweep the Series.

The All-Star Game

As a result of the shrinking revenue in baseball, a new promotion came into the game. The All-Star Game was the brainchild of *Chicago Tribune* sports editor, Arch Ward, to acknowledge the city's "Century of Progress International Exposition" in Comiskey Park, Chicago, July 6, 1933. (3). What a thrill it was for the fans to see the best players that the game had to offer play on the same field. Revenue generated for this annual event came around in turn to each city in the Major Leagues.

In addition to the All-Star game itself, (a different city would spon-sor the All-Star Game every year after that), the "Home Run Derby" later became a big attraction in 1985. The Derby played on the night before the All-Star Game and has become so popular that it attracts sell-out crowds. Mets slugger Pete Alonzo, in 2019, won the latest con-test. From his prize of $1,000,000, he generously donated five-percent of his wind-fall to the Wounded Warrior Project (benefitting returning United States veterans who have sustained psychological and physical injuries) and five-percent to the Tunnel to Towers Project (in honor of the sacrifices of the first responders and military heroes in response to the 9/11 attack).

Night Baseball and Radio

The owners needed to try new methods to attract fans. Gradually, the teams that were somewhat reluctant to expand their fan base through radio broadcasts were more eager now to take a big step. They permitted live broadcasts. Although the Negro Leagues held primacy of introduc-ing night games, unofficial night exhibitions played from 1920 to 1927. Independence, Kansas, hosted the first professional night game. The first major league team to host games at night came about on the evening of May 24, 1935, when President Franklin Roosevelt symbolically flipped a switch in Washington, D.C., that lit up Ohio's Crosley Field, home of the Cincinnati Reds. (4)

Some cities, like New York, kept a moratorium on radio broadcasting until 1939. There were some exceptions to the New York radio ban. A few opening days and other scattered games aired. All-Star games and the World Series were broadcasted on New York radio stations. However, New Yorkers were unable to hear Major League Baseball games regularly until Larry MacPhail, who was brought to New York from the Cincinnati Reds to take over the operation of a moribund Brooklyn Dodger franchise, broke the radio blackout in 1939. (5)

Hank Greenberg
Courtesy - Hall of Fame

To the credit of the game, while thousands of banks closed during the 1930s, and, as millions of people lost their jobs, baseball still survived. No franchises went under, nor were there relocations of the clubs during the Depression.

Ethnicity

During the Depression, the success of the Yankees and the Cubs helped the weaker teams survive at the gate with their drawing power. Starting in 1936, future Hall of Famer Joe DiMaggio arrived in New York to join the Yankees and helped the team win an unprecedented four consecutive World Series from 1936-1939 in beating the Giants twice, the Cubs, and the Cincinnati Reds. Joe DiMaggio's persona both on and off the field exuded class. His Italian-American heritage gave hope to the struggling immigrants who were seeking the "pot-of-gold" here in America.

Bronx native, future Hall of Famer, Hank Greenberg, was likewise a hero to the large Jewish population in New York as ethnicity began to play a more significant role in baseball. Over the years, the different ethnic groups accepted into Major League players' ranks were Irish, German, Polish, Italian, followed by Hispanic, and Black toward the middle of the century. (6)

Lately, there has been an influx of Japanese and Korean ballplayers coming into the Major Leagues and, to a lesser degree, ballplayers from Australia—all resulting from baseball's globalization.

The Hall of Fame

By decree from the 1907 Mills Commission, Abner Doubleday created the game of baseball on an idyllic field upstate in Cooperstown, New York. For this reason, the Baseball Hall of Fame was established in Cooperstown in 1936. Election into the Hall of Fame has become a great honor for players of the game since then. The town of Cooperstown has become a mecca not only for the players but also for avid baseball fans arriving from all over to partake in the elaborate induction ceremonies. The first inductees were announced in 1936, and, yes, Babe Ruth was on the original list.

As the story goes, Steven Clark (1882-1960), a wealthy Cooperstown businessman and heir to the Singer Sewing machine fortune, collected the baseball memorabilia that formed the core of the original materials in the Hall. The display included an old baseball that purportedly was, as earlier stated, found in an old trunk and supposedly was the ball used by Abner Doubleday in the first base ball game in 1839. It is still on display at the Hall. (7)

On the strength of this story and in honor of the game's centennial, the doors of the Hall of Fame officially opened on June 12, 1939, in that small-town setting of Cooperstown, New York. To commemorate this major event, a speech given by Baseball Commissioner Kenesaw Mountain Landis, he stated, "Since for a hundred years this game of baseball has lived and thrived and spread all over our country and a large part of the world, it is fitting that it should have a National Museum. And nowhere else than its birthplace could this museum be appropriately situated," later stated Bert Sugar in his book, *Bert Sugar's Baseball Hall of Fame; A History of America's Greatest Game.* (8)

Lou Gehrig

One of the best-loved ballplayers, Yankee first baseman Lou Gehrig, left the game after recording 2,130 consecutive games. After a steady decline in his play, in 1939, Gehrig was diagnosed with Amyotrophic Lateral Sclerosis disease, which causes the autonomic nervous system to deteriorate. Daniel Slotnik, *The New York Times,* wrote on Nov. 9, 2017:

> **One undeniably superhuman moment of Gehrig's career was his farewell speech at Yankee Stadium on July 4, 1939. Mr. (Bojangles) Robinson who was there and called the speech "baseball's Gettysburg Address," told The Daily News in 2014 that the sound system made it hard to make out all of Gehrig's words, but that an almost religious solemnity descended over the stadium as Gehrig spoke. (9)**

On July 4, 1939, Lou Gehrig delivered one of the most famous speeches in American history in Yankee Stadium with a sellout crowd of over 61,000 people in attendance:

One of the greatest speeches in American history!
Courtesy - Library of Congress

Fans, for the past two weeks you have been reading about the bad break I got. Yet today I consider myself the luckiest man

on the face of this Earth. I have been in ballparks for seventeen years and have never received anything but kindness and encouragement from you fans. Look at these grand men. Which of you wouldn't consider it the highlight of his career just to associate with them for even one day? Sure, I'm lucky. Who wouldn't consider it an honor to have known Jacob Ruppert? Also, the builder of baseball's greatest empire, Ed Barrow? To have spent six years with that wonderful little fellow, Miller Huggins? Then to have spent the next nine years with that outstanding leader, that smart student of psychology, the best manager in baseball today, Joe McCarthy? Sure, I'm lucky. When the New York Giants, a team you would give your right arm to beat, and vice versa, sends you a gift—that's something. When everybody down to the groundskeepers and those boys in white coats remember you with trophies— that's something. When you have a wonderful mother-in-law who takes sides with you in squabbles with her own daughter—that's something. When you have a father and a mother who work all their lives so you can have an education and build your body—it's a blessing. When you have a wife who has been a tower of strength and shown more courage than you dreamed existed—that's the finest I know. So, I close in saying that I may have had a tough break, but I have an awful lot to live for." (10)

In less than two years, Gehrig would succumb to ALS, also called Lou Gehrig's Disease.

CHAPTER 11

The War Years

a. 1941

b. Joe DiMaggio and Ted Williams

c. World War II and the Green Light Letter

d. Women in Baseball

e. The Aftermath and Baseball's Great Experiment

1941

Many claimed that the year 1941 was the greatest in baseball history. The impact and on-going suspense of the dramas that unfolded day after day was palpable. The looming winds of war to Joe DiMaggio's 56 game hitting streak, Ted Williams' dramatic home run ending the All-Star game and his successful bid for a .400 batting average, and the first thrilling Dodgers and Yankees World Series made for an exciting 1941 season. Of course, the Japanese attack on Pearl Harbor on December 7, 1941, and the recently passed draft laws affected the players. People were on edge as they heard President Franklin D. Roosevelt's radio fireside chats claiming how important it was to the United States to be concerned about the devastation in Great Britain as a result of the constant Luftwaffe bombings. Robert Creamer, In *Baseball and Other Matters* in 1941. (1)

Joe DiMaggio and Ted Williams

Nineteen forty-one was the third year that New York City listened to baseball games on the radio. After winning four consecutive World Series, the New York Yankees faded in 1940. They looked to correct that misstep in 1941. Even though the winds of war beckoned, baseball threatened to take away the newspaper headlines from the world crisis as the season moved on. One of the greatest stars in baseball, Yankees centerfielder Joe DiMaggio, began making the headlines in the daily newspapers by building a modest hitting streak in May. And, Boston Red Sox left fielder, Ted Williams, was vying for the same headlines as he was hitting toward the elusive .400 batting average, which was truly phenomenal. Attesting to the character of Ted Williams in his chase for the coveted .400 BA by getting six hits in his final two games to ensure the title. These two stars were taking top billing in the news as they courted their streaks. Ed Rielly, in his book, *Baseball and American Culture,* eloquently stated, "Not only do these names call forth great ballplayers of the past, but images of American heroes, images of what it means to be American."(2)

During Joe DiMaggio's 56-game hitting streak, cries of, "what did he do, what did he do?" and "Did he get a hit?" were questions asked by people in cities across the country, especially in New York City, where the many appliance stores hawked their radios in the store windows with the game on. One could hear the whole game, pitch by pitch, walking block after block in midtown Manhattan.

With the record climbing to 56 games, the New York Yankees were playing the Cleveland Indians in their Municipal Stadium that holds the largest capacity in the Major Leagues. The game drew over 67,000 people when DiMaggio's streak ended on a couple of great defensive plays.

However, baseball drama continued on July 8 as the best players of both leagues vied for the bragging rights in the All-Star Game held in Detroit. With the National League-leading 5-4 going into the bottom of the ninth inning with two men on base and two outs, the great Ted Williams hit a dramatic game-ending home run.

Perhaps a little less dramatic than Joe DiMaggio's record-breaking hitting streak earlier in the season, Williams was still flirting with a .400 batting average until the last game when he broke through the .400 barrier. Twenty-one years after the Brooklyn Robins were in postseason play, they climbed back up to the top by playing the New York Yankees in the World Series, the fall classic. Having a city's team in the World Series is great for that city as excitement builds for this event, and post-season play brings more revenue. But when there are two teams from the same city involved, it is a veritable boon to that city. With fans drawn from both leagues and the banter between the two sides and their fans so intense, the additional revenue helped fill the city's coffers. Benjamin Rader wrote, "Representative professional baseball teams exhibited a remarkable capacity for giving cities and towns deeper emotional existences: teams helped define the particular character of an urban community, providing citizens with a great sense of place and sharply delineated collective memories." (3) The Brooklyn Dodgers exhibited this sense of community like no other team. Besides their distinctive dialect, the Dodgers' fans ascribed to a different culture.

Through the years, there were sideshows such as "Shorty" Laurice and his Symphoney [sic] band that entertained the crowd at Ebbets Field, the Dodgers' home, with their rendition of "Three Blind Mice" as the umpires were entering the field of play. Hilda Chester ringing her cowbell was a fixture at Dodger games, and Happy Felton hosted a kid's television show called the "Knothole Gang" live from

Ebbets Field. All this was played out in a bandbox of a ballpark with a capacity of only 32,000 for *Dem Bums* as the Dodger players were affectionately known. (4) The nickname "Dem Bums" along with "Basement Bertha," were an a to caricutres drawn by the *Daily News* cartoonist, Willard Mullins. Furthermore, many of the Dodgers lived in the community, leading to the mutual enchantment between the players and their fans.

Unfortunately for the Dodgers, as they were about to tie the World Series in 1941 at two games apiece in the top of the ninth inning, the Yankees' batter reached base through an error on the Dodger catcher's part enabling the inning to continue. The Yankees went on to win the game and then closed out the Series with a victory in the next game. Brooklyn, however, was back on the map.

World War II and the Green Light Letter

A month after the attack on Pearl Harbor on December 7, 1941, Baseball Commissioner Kenesaw Mountain Landis, concerned about the position of baseball in regard to the war, wrote a letter to President Roosevelt. In it, he wrote, "The time is approaching when, in ordinary conditions, our teams would be heading for spring training camps. However, since these are not ordinary times, I venture to ask what you have in mind as to whether professional baseball should continue to operate."

President Roosevelt responded that he "honestly [felt] that it would be best for the country to keep baseball going." The president continued saying that, "even if the greater use of older players lowers the actual quality of the teams, this will not dampen the popularity of the sport." (5)

Below is an image of President Roosevelt's full response to Commissioner (Judge) Landis:

THE WHITE HOUSE
WASHINGTON

January 15, 1942.

My dear Judge:-

Thank you for yours of January fourteenth. As you will, of course, realize the final decision about the baseball season must rest with you and the Baseball Club owners -- so what I am going to say is solely a personal and not an official point of view.

I honestly feel that it would be best for the country to keep baseball going. There will be fewer people unemployed and everybody will work longer hours and harder than ever before.

And that means that they ought to have a chance for recreation and for taking their minds off their work even more than before.

Baseball provides a recreation which does not last over two hours or two hours and a half, and which can be got for very little cost. And, incidentally, I hope that night games can be extended because it gives an opportunity to the day shift to see a game occasionally.

As to the players themselves, I know you agree with me that individual players who are of active military or naval age should go, without question, into the services. Even if the actual quality of the teams is lowered by the greater use of older players, this will not dampen the popularity of the sport. Of course, if any individual has some particular aptitude in a trade or profession, he ought to serve the Government. That, however, is a matter which I know you can handle with complete justice.

Here is another way of looking at it -- if 300 teams use 5,000 or 6,000 players, these players are a definite recreational asset to at least 20,000,000 of their fellow citizens -- and that in my judgment is thoroughly worthwhile.

With every best wish,

Very sincerely yours,

Franklin D. Roosevelt

Hon. Kenesaw M. Landis,
333 North Michigan Avenue,
Chicago,
Illinois.

Courtesy - Library of Congress

Over 500 Major League ballplayers and 5,000 Minor Leaguers enlisted in the World War II war effort. Unfortunately, some did not return, and others sustained injuries in combat. The Major Leaguers who saw heavy fighting included Ralph Houk and Warren Spahn in the Battle of the Bulge and Yogi Berra, who provided fire support for the Marines landing at the

During World War II, the ballplayers involved in the country's service around the globe did their best to replicate the playing fields during recreation. This photo taken at Camp Marshall in Lyautey, Morocco, North Africa
Courtesy - Hall of Fame

Normandy beachhead. Jerry Coleman, a Marine pilot, flew 120 sorties as a dive bomber in World War II, and later in the Korean War. Ted Williams, who served in World War II, also flew combat missions in the Korean War. Joe DiMaggio, Bob Feller, and Hank Greenberg also served their country. Greenberg was declared unfit for duty two days before December 7, 1941, after initially enlisting for duty. After the attack on Pearl Harbor, he re-enlisted for combat duty. And Dodger, Moe Berg, catcher, and spy, was highly touted by the NYC Jewish neighborhoods as was Hank Greenberg. These players and others provided countless acts of bravery for the love of the country. (6)

Women in Baseball

During World War II, many of the Major and Minor League ballplayers had committed to the war effort, thus reducing the talent of their teams. An astute businessman, Phil Wrigley, chewing gum magnate and

Chicago Cubs owner, entertained ideas to supplant the loss of 40 percent of those Major Leaguers to the war effort. Plus, the draft claimed many 18-year-old young men, decimating the minor leagues. Wrigley looked to the mid-western cities that focused on the war industry. (7) As reported by Bill Francis of the National Baseball Hall of Fame:

> **The AAGPBL, which began play in 1943 and lasted a dozen years, gave more than 500 women an opportunity that had never existed before. Popularized by the 1992 feature film A League of Their Own ("There's no crying in baseball!"), the so-called "lipstick league" was the brainchild of Chicago Cubs owner Philip K. Wrigley as a way to keep the ballparks busy during World War II if manpower shortages threatened big league baseball. (8)**

At this time, one patriotic symbol was the playing of the national anthem before every baseball game. By 1945 sports, both amateur and professional, followed baseball's lead and opened each game with "*The Star-Spangled Banner*." The new booming public address systems that came into play by 1945 enhanced this practice. (9)

The Aftermath and the Great Experiment

In *Much More than a Game*, Robert F. Burk wrote,

> **"The war exacted a heavy toll on Organized Baseball's gate. Major League attendance, which had struggled back to 18.5 million in 1939, fell to under 8 million in 1943 and only rebounded to 11 million by 1945 as veterans slowly returned to the ballfields. The minors were more severely damaged." (10)**

Attendance boomed again in the postwar glow. The highpoint of this period came in 1947 with baseball's breaking of the color barrier as the

Brooklyn Dodgers brought on Jackie Robinson to play first base in what was termed the "Great Experiment" he became the majors' first black ball-player since Moses "Fleetwood" Walker in 1887. Integration now had every opportunity to succeed. For one, after the passing of Commissioner Landis, his replacement, Albert Benjamin "Happy" Chandler, opened the door. The great feeling of crushing the Axis powers in the war encouraged a brighter future not only in baseball but in America's popular culture.

Additionally, the foundation laid for the current Major League Baseball Players' Association (MLBPA) through the players' organization called the American Baseball Guild commenced in 1947. A maximum pay cut of 25 percent, a minimum salary of $5,000, a promise to create a pension plan, and $25 per week in living expenses for spring training camp was demanded. Until 1947, players received only expense money for spring training. (11)

Concurrently, the Latino community re-entered baseball as a result of the integration.

CHAPTER 12

New York's Glory Days (1947-1957)

---

a. The Golden Era of New York City Baseball

b. Babe Ruth Day

c. The Negro League (Robinson vs. Manley)

d. The Great Rivalry

e. O'Malley vs. Moses

f. Exodus

The Golden Era of New York City Baseball

Baseball witnessed the illustrious history of New York City teams reach its height from 1947 to 1957. During that period, the Yankees were participants in the World Series nine times, winning seven times; the Dodgers were participants six times and won one championship with the Giants involved in two World Series, winning once.

Arguably, the greatest intra-city rivalry in professional sports during the twentieth century was between the Brooklyn Dodgers and the New York Yankees. Brooklyn incorporated as the City of Brooklyn in 1834. In 1838 the Green-Wood Cemetery opened. In 1859, the Brooklyn Academy of Music formed. Prospect Park opened in 1867 and one of Brooklyn's, and for that matter, one of the country's most famous landmarks, the

Brooklyn Bridge, opened in 1883. Creating a Greater New York involved a variety of factors—political, economic, social, sectional, and selfish. Ultimately, an act of the State Legislature was signed into law on May 14, 1897, calling for consolidation of the five boroughs on January 1, 1898, thus giving the city a new charter. (1) Many Brooklynites felt that they would lose their identity with this consolidation, a notion that persisted well into the twentieth century.

Through the first couple of decades of the twentieth century, the only consistently competitive team in town was the New York Giants. That all changed when Babe Ruth came to New York, and the Brooklyn Robins went to the World Series in 1920, though Brooklyn lost that year. The name "Dodgers" formally appeared in 1932. Significant changes came especially for the Dodgers in 1941, as they won the National League Pennant and then went on to the World Series to play the Yankees. Total euphoria would be the best way to describe the feeling of the Brooklynites at that time.

Integration was a watershed moment in America's history, not only for African Americans but for other oppressed people who benefited from this moment. However, seldom do we hear about the cost involved in this groundbreaking event. Robert Cvornyek wrote an excellent informative essay titled "Redefining the Narrative—Effa Manley, Jackie Robinson, and the Integration of Baseball" to be included in the book *Baseball in the Classroom* by Ed Rielly.

Opening day, April 15, 1947, witnessed the long-awaited integration of baseball. Arthur Daley wrote in *The New York Times* the following day:

> **Did one notice, by the way, the deft manner in which the deacon of the Dodgers, Branch Rickey, brought up Robinson? He practically smuggled him in. Just as the excitement of the Durocher episode reached its apex, Ricky quietly announced that Jackie signed to a Dodger contract. (2) Thus, did he hope that the precedent-shattering implications of Robbie's promotion would be smothered by the publicity engendered by Leo Durocher's suspension? The 'Unobtrusive Entrance' is merely an attempt to lighten the pressure on Robinson's shoulders. (3)**

Babe Ruth Day

Louis Efrat, The *New York Times*, April 27th, 1947, wrote:

> **At Baseball Commissioner Happy Chandler's request, the New**
> **York Yankees hosted "Babe Ruth Day," a national event to**
> **honor the baseball legend who was suffering the debilitating**
> **effects of nasopharyngeal cancer. He was greeted by 58,339 fans**
> **that day in the "House That Ruth Built," and the ceremony**
> **and speeches were fed into every Major and Minor League sta-**
> **dium. According to the New York Times, "Just before he spoke,**
> **Ruth started to cough, and it appeared that he might break**
> **down because of the thunderous cheers that came his way. But**
> **once he started to talk, he was all right, still the champion. It**
> **was the many men who surrounded him on the field, players,**
> **newspaper and radio persons, who choked up." (4)**

The fact that he never forgot his upbringing in St. Mary's Industrial Home for Boys in Baltimore, Maryland, contributed to his greatest achievements. Throughout his life, he gave his time and resources to acknowledge the needs of youngsters. The Babe appeared at their homes, at hospitals, on the streets, or in the ballpark, a great tribute from a great man. The Babe finally succumbed to the ravages of throat cancer on August 16, 1948. His bier was available for the public to pay their respects to him by Gate Four in Yankee Stadium. Over 100,000 people paid homage to the Babe over two days. Babe Ruth became a larger than life figure in America's popular culture for more than one hundred years.

The Negro League (Robinson vs. Manley)

It was a glorious day for baseball and American culture as new doors opened, and some old doors were knocked down when Jackie Robinson signed with the Dodgers. The corporate atmosphere touted individual achievement and teamwork, and that is the essence of what baseball is all about. This mani-festo does not permit discrimination as it limits the potential for more excep-tional business. Furthermore, President Truman integrated the armed forces through a decree in 1948. Hence, the Major Leagues experienced a boon at that time. The main drawback of this period of integration was that as the American League and the National League rapidly expanded, they sapped the Negro Leagues of their greater ballplayers with no compensation and, in a short period decimated attendance at their games.

To make matters worse, in an interview with *Ebony* magazine, Robinson praised integration and denigrated the Negro Leagues as an "unprofessional operation that compromised the integrity of its ball-players and fans," stated Negro baseball historian, Roberta Newman. (5) In exposing all their warts, Jackie's opposition hurt and embittered Effa Manley, the owner of the Newark Eagles of the Negro National League. She made a valiant and legitimate effort in claiming that Branch Rickey "stole" the best Negro League ballplayer without offering any compensation to the club for its the loss.

In 1942, Kenesaw Mountain Landis had issued a statement deny-ing that there was a written agreement to keep Blacks out of the Major Leagues. He said, "The only obstacle that had barred blacks from play-ing was a 'gentlemen's agreement,' which operated on a matter of principle." Was social justice observed and served as Rickey broke this pact? This state of affairs begs the question, "is Negro baseball now doomed?" Did the Negro Leagues help audition talent for the Major Leagues? Was it worth saving the Negro Leagues for reasons of this nature? In *Black Baseball, Black Business,* Roberta Newman wrote:

Keeping black baseball as an ongoing concern, however, would require a substantial retrenchment as well as a consid-erable definition of the baseball model itself. The final decade of organized Black baseball would demonstrate the extent to which changes in the game, as well as the economic climate, affected urban enclaves with the stake in Black baseball. With

integration on the rise, however slowly, the segregated dollar could no longer play a central role in the business of the African American, and Black baseball stood squarely on the border between the past and the future. (6)

Former Negro National League (NNL) ballplayer Jim Robinson played with and starred for the Kansas City Monarchs from 1956 - 1958. He was a graduate of North Carolina A & T and a Korean War veteran. Jim spoke warmly of the inspiration that he got through his friendship with three-time Brooklyn Dodger Most Valuable Player, Roy Campanella, in a telephone interview in July 2019.

Unfortunately, the Yankees and many other ballclubs were also slow to integrate. It was evident that the Yankees' success was there already. So, in effect, why would they disturb that formula? However, it would have resonated a great deal more if the premier team in baseball placed its stamp of approval much earlier on integration than when they eventually did by hiring Elston Howard in 1955 as the first Black player for the Yankees. Howard was also the first Black ballplayer to be voted as Most Valuable Player (MVP) in the American League. The Yankees were 13th out of the 16 teams in hiring Negro ballplayers. In an interview with the foremost Negro League authority, John Holway, in July of 2019, he stressed "the importance of keeping the NNL alive and thriving as integration into the National and American leagues at the time moved glacially. For example, the Boston Red Sox did not integrate until 1959."

The Latino Influence

Concurrently, integration also opened the door for the Latino ballplayer. According to the data compiled by Alex Butler of UPI in 2019:

"By 1981, 18.7 percent of MLB players were African Americans. But by 2017, only 6.7 percent of MLB players were African Americans. While the number of African Americans

in the league fell, the number of Latino players began to rise. Latino players replaced African American players as the second most dominant race/ethnicity in MLB by 1993. By 2017, 27.4 percent of MLB players were Latinos."

The US Census Bureau reported the Latino population in New York City climbed from 152,271 in 1950 to 2,426,013 making up 29.1% of the city's total of the first two decades in the 20th Century. -**https://www. pewresearch.org/fact-tank/**

The Great Rivalries

In 1949, two of the greatest rivalries in professional sports came to the biggest stage in baseball—New York. The highly charged competition between the Boston Red Sox and the New York Yankees did not start in 1903 when the Red Sox and the Yankees (née Highlanders) went into the final days of the season with the pennant on the line. We cannot qualify this as a rivalry though the Red Sox went on to defeat the Yankees in those final games of the season for the American League pennant and then went on to win their first World Series against the Pittsburgh Pirates.

There may be a little justification to state that the rivalry between the two teams had roots in the early nineteenth century when two separate forms of baseball, the "Massachusetts" game, and the "New York" game, were both vying for respectability. By the middle of the 19th century, the New York game, advanced by the rules of the New York Knickerbockers, predominated, eliminating the Massachusetts game. The Red Sox won the World Series four more times during the next decade, (1912, 15,16, and 18), as the Yankees were pretty much ineffective. On an aside, ironically, the Red Sox won another four championships a century later in the first two decades (2004,07,13, and 18).

The first true rivalry between the Red Sox and the Yankees emerged in 1920 as Boston, stung from the wounds of losing their greatest ballplayer, Babe Ruth, to the New York Yankees. Ruth then led the Yankees to seven American League pennants and four World Series championships as he was embracing the "Roarin' 20s." Meanwhile, Boston was floundering in the lower depths of the American League until the middle of the 1940s when they finally acquired the talent to bring them back into contention. It would be eighty-six years passed (1918-2004), between championships, including heart-breaking losses during that stretch. Boston sportswriter, Dan "Red" Shaughnessy, wrote a book titled "The Curse of the Bambino," detailing the travails of the Red Sox ineptitude during that long stretch after a particularly tough loss in the 1986 World Series to the New York Mets. They did avenge some of their hardships by beating the New York Yankees in a thrilling come-from-behind victory in the American League Championship Series in 2004, propelling them to their first Championship since 1918. In that year, their star pitcher and their star slugger was none other than Babe Ruth.

A sub-plot to this excitement was the question of who was the better ballplayer—Joe DiMaggio or Ted Williams. Although the press had a field day with this, rivalry the two stars were real friends who also shared good times off the field. Nevertheless, the rivalry started to take hold. Unfortunately for the Bostonians, the Yankees reached their heyday of success as they went on to win fourteen pennants, including ten World Series in eighteen years, a truly phenomenal run. The Red Sox failed to make the Series through that whole stretch.

Intracity rivalries began at the beginning of the twentieth century. In two decades, the Giants were always in contention for World Series play by winning eleven pennants and three World Series during that period, while the Brooklyn team had won just once. The Yankees were pretty much a non-entity then. An intracity rivalry developed in 1921 when the Giants and Yankees met in the World Series three consecutive times as they vied for the heart and soul of New York City. The Giants took two out of the three series in 1921 and 1922. By then, Babe Ruth's star was shining brightly with the Yankees, and they won their first World Series victory over the Giants in 1923. Attendance spiked as Babe Ruth brought a new dimension into the game with his dynamic home runs. The Brooklyn Dodgers, (a.k.a., the Superbas), participated in the World Series in 1890, and then known as the Robins in 1916 and 1920, losing both those times.

In 1941, the old Brooklyn-New York rivalry returned with great intensity. The Dodgers won the National League pennant as the Yankees won the American League pennant. The strength of this intra-city rivalry heated up in 1947 when Jackie Robinson, who was to become Rookie of the Year, led the Dodgers to the top of the National League at the end of the season only to face the power-laden New York Yankees in the fall classic. Integration intensified this match-up to the nth degree as Robinson taunted the Yankees pitchers with his daring base running. Jackie was always a threat to steal a base, and, in some cases, he stole home plate. The Yankees beat the Dodgers in seven exciting games to win the '47 World Series. It was also the beginning of the "Golden Era in New York City Baseball" (1947-1957). In those eleven years, either the Giants, the Dodgers or the Yankees went to the World Series (except for one season, 1948), making for a lot of happy New York baseball fans.

Through the years, many have questioned why it took the Yankees eight years before they fully integrated by bringing up a great catcher by the name of Elston Howard. During that time, the Yankees won six World Series, at one point winning five fall classics in a row from 1949-1953. Adding, Glenn Stout, stated in his *Yankees Century"*

No team was in a better position to capitalize on this than the Yankees. Because of Ruth, [Ruth was a big proponent of the Negro League ballplayers] the Yankees were, before Robinson signed, the de facto favorites of Black America. Few teams could match their financial resources, and in Newark, Kansas City, and New York, the Yankees already rented their ballparks to Negro League clubs. The Yankees had an inside track signing Negro League players from these teams if they chose to. (7)

In 1950, the Yankees won the American League pennant, and then they swept the Philadelphia Phillies 4-0 in the World Series. After making a derogatory comment to Yankees co-owner Del Webb, Commissioner Happy Chandler got a no-confidence vote on his contract renewal and was ousted. Before departing, Chandler sealed a deal with the Gillette Safety Razor Company for $6 million over six years to televise the annual All-Star Game, the proceeds of which would benefit the players' pension fund. (8)

One of the most memorable comebacks in baseball history started in the middle of August of 1951 as the Brooklyn Dodgers had a 13 and one-half game lead on the New York Giants. The call-up of a twenty-year old rookie named Willie Mays energized the Giants The team started a comeback that led them to catch up to the Dodgers at season's end, a truly miraculous feat. In the end, all three New York teams had a chance at playing in the World Series, but only two teams could make it. Many said that this was the most exciting season in baseball's history. With both the Giants and the Dodgers having the same record, it necessitated a three-game playoff to determine which team would go to the World Series to play the Yankees.

In the third and final game, the Dodgers built a three-run lead in the top of the eighth inning to make the score 4-1 in their favor. A press box announcement came across the loudspeaker: "All accredited writers should pick up press passes for tomorrow's World Series game at Ebbets Field. Passes will be distributed in the Dodger clubhouse until 5:00 p.m." (9) In the bottom of the ninth inning with one run across making the score 4-2 with one out and two men on base, the Giants Bobby Thomson stepped up to the plate. Giants' announcer Russ Hodges described the event over WMCA Radio:

"Bobby Thomson up there swinging... He's had a single and double and drove in the Giants first run with a long fly to center. Branca pitches and Bobby takes a strike call on the inside corner. Bobby hitting at .292 that he's had a single

and double and drove in the Giants first run with a long fly to center ... Brooklyn leads it 4-2. Hartung down the line at third not taking any chances. Lockman without too big a lead at second, but he will be running like the wind if Thomson hits one. Branca throws. There's a long drive, it's gonna be I believe the Giants win the pennant! The Giants win the pennant! The Giants win the pennant! Bobby Thompson hits into the lower deck of the left-field stands!... The Giants win the pennant, and they're going crazy!... Yahoo-o-o-o!!!"[sic](10)

This singular most historic and dramatic event claimed to have the comeback tainted during that thrilling run that the Giants had in August and September of 1951. At the Society of American Baseball Research meeting in Westchester County, New York, the backup Giants' catcher, guest speaker, Sal Yvars, acknowledged that there was sign-stealing by the Giants. Yvars claimed that there was a person with a high-powered telescope in the centerfield clubhouse who would read the signals from the opposing catcher as to what pitch would be thrown. He would then relay that pitch to a player in the bullpen who would then flash a sign to the Giants' batter as to what to expect on the next pitch. Other Giants corroborated these allegations as the story came public in 1961. The Yankees then beat the Giants in the World Series four games to two for their third consecutive World Series victory. Nothing more was heard about any sign-stealing at that time. (11)

In the post-season, Jackie Robinson, appearing on the NBC program *Youth Want to Know*, ignited controversy with incendiary remarks claiming that the Yankees were blind because there were no blacks on their team and very few in their Minor League system. "It seems to me that the Yankees' front office has used racial prejudice in its dealing with Negro ballplayers." Robinson then walked it back to a degree, stating, "I may be wrong, but the Yankees will have to prove it to me," reported Richard McElvey in his book, *The MacPhail's: baseball's first family of the front office.* (12) These are harsh allegations in any case. Yankees general manager George Weiss responded that there were "numerous" blacks in the system. McKelvey added, "It has always been our hope that one of these shall prove good enough to make it with the Yankees. However, we do not intend under any circumstances to bring one up just for exploitation." (13)

After seventy-seven years, the Boston Braves, who recently played in the 1948 World Series, moved to Milwaukee in March of 1953. It was the first National League shift since 1900. Following a steep loss of $700,000 in 1952, the Braves went on to top the Major Leagues in attendance in 1953. In the following year, the St. Louis Browns were purchased by a Baltimore syndicate and became the Baltimore Orioles. (14) And in 1955, the Philadelphia Athletics transferred to Kansas City. By this time, air travel began to replace the railroad as the principal means of transportation. And, with the jet age taking hold, the rapidly growing west coast beckoned for baseball. Two years later, the Giants and the Dodgers moved westward. The Dodgers finally beat the New York Yankees in the thrilling 1955 World Series after losing their five previous World Series attempts when they played each other.

O'Malley vs. Moses

The Milwaukee move was not lost on Dodgers' owner Walter O'Malley. He was genuinely concerned that the pennant-winning Dodgers saw a drop-off of 200,000 attendees in 1952. Aware of the success of the Milwaukee Braves, O'Malley, convinced that drastic changes were necessary to continue playing in Ebbets Field. (15) Eventually, Milwaukee would rise to the top of the National League, winning it all in 1957 by beating the Yankees in the World Series.

In 1955, O'Malley approached the city for a new domed stadium to be built as a public conveyance in the Flatlands section of Brooklyn in the area that Barclays Center would eventually be built. However, Robert Moses, the ultimate "power broker" in the city as the Commissioner of Parks and Recreation, was adamantly opposed to O'Malley's request. Moses offered to build a multi-purpose stadium in Flushing, Queens fell on O'Malley's deaf ears.

On the surface, O'Malley had a legitimate request in building a new ballpark in that 40-year-old Ebbets Field had a limited capacity of 32,000 and was in dire need of more seating capacity and better aisles plus the old seats were uncomfortable. The irony here was the fact that during this period of the Golden Era of New York City baseball, the Brooklyn Dodgers were the most successful team. (16)

Unfortunately for O'Malley and the Dodgers, their pleas were stonewalled by Robert Moses, perhaps the most powerful man at the time who did not hold an elected position. Parks, parkways, beaches, low-middle income housing, and interstate highways all came under his purview. He had no concern about a baseball team, especially one that belonged to O'Malley. The two men never got along well enough to compromise on any facet. Furthermore, not even NYC Mayor Robert Wagner agreed to O'Malley's requests. The debates went on ad nauseum as to who precipitated the Dodgers' departure. Nevertheless, in the prophetic words of the great sage and soothsayer, A. Bartlett Giamatti, "The city dies when industry flees. The neighborhoods are the vital cells of the urban organism." (17)

With the Dodgers losing to the New York Yankees for the third time in the Yankees' unprecedented winning streak of five consecutive World Series Championships, from 1949-1953, there were rumors of the team moving. Their first and only World Series win in exciting1955 after five previous losses to the New York Yankees did not change O'Malley's mind about moving the Dodgers away from their faithful fans through all of those tough years.

Exodus

The first inkling of O'Malley's interest in Los Angeles came about when he invited Kenneth Hahn, a member of the Los Angeles Board of Supervisors, to the 1956 World Series. The New York Yankees beat them for the sixth time. Hahn later explained that O'Malley was actively seeking to leave Brooklyn. When the Dodgers headed to Japan for an exhibition tour, they stopped off in Los Angeles. O'Malley took a tour of Chavez Ravine, the potential site for a ballpark, and by the end of the tour, O'Malley and Hahn virtually had a deal.

A Perfect Game in the 1956 World Series
Courtesy - Library of Congress

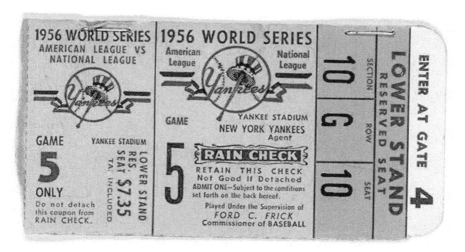

Courtesy - Library of Congress

Two matters had to be considered. First, the Dodgers had to buy the rights to the Los Angeles area owned by the Cubs. Cubs owner Phil Wrigley was not happy with his treatment in LA, so it was not a difficult task for O'Malley to "take it off his hands." (18) Second, then Major League Baseball Commissioner, Ford Frick, would not allow just one team to head west. The Giants had been looking to move since 1955, while playing second-fiddle to the Dodgers in the National League and the high-flying Yankees less than a mile away who decimated their fan base. It was a no-brainer for O'Malley to convince Giants' owner Horace Stoneham to bring his team west with him. (19)

History does tend to repeat itself! If we go back 170 years to the "gold rush" in 1849, people followed the Santa Fe Trail, the Oregon Trail, the Old Spanish Trail, the Mormon Trail, and the California Trail to go westward. That is not much different than what the baseball trailblazers, O'Malley, and Stoneham, accomplished when they moved their teams west. Again, we witness a "Manifest Destiny."

CHAPTER 13

Expansion

a. The Continental League
b. Expansion and Relocation
c. Marvin Miller and The Players Union
d. Curt Flood
e. A Man on the Moon and the Mets Win It All

The 1960s witnessed civil rights movements causing racial unrest in the form of riots and arson in the cities. The "police action" in Vietnam took hold in the middle of the decade, and the assassinations of Martin Luther King, Jr. for the tv viewers at home for, "as the television viewers at home watched the news in horror."

The Continental League

After the Yankees lost the World Series to the Milwaukee Braves in 1957, they rebounded in 1958 to win it all. This joyous occasion did not assuage the feelings of the National League fans in New York. The departure of the two National League teams after the 1957 season was a crushing blow to the city and its baseball fans. Also, it was a significant economic loss to New York. Attorney William Shea was asked by the city to bring a desperately needed team to New York, and baseball guru Branch Rickey proposed to operate a new league, the "Continental League." They gathered signatories from eight cities to participate.

The proposed league was to meet on August 18, 1960, with Major League Baseball Commissioner Ford Frick and his committee. However, the meeting never occurred since Major League Baseball announced that it would expand by four teams, two in the National League and two in the American League two weeks before the meeting, thus, rendering the meeting useless. (1) Ultimately, the National upheld its promise by awarding the Continental League two teams, but the American League did not keep its commitment. In a letter to Branch Rickey, M. Donald Grant, (representing Mets' owner, Joan Payson), and the manuscript division of the Library of Congress, it stated:

The Continental League died on August 2, 1960, and William Shea was pleased, but not completely satisfied. On that date, representatives of the NL and the AL promised Shea that each League would accept two of the CL franchises. The NL upheld its promise by granting Houston and New York expansion teams for the 1962 season, and Shea received his reward by having the Mets' new stadium named after him. However, the AL reneged by ignoring other CL investors and instead voted Los Angeles and Washington (to replace the original Senators, who fled to Minneapolis, a CL city) into the League for the 1961 season. (2)

Expansion and Relocation

Enough cities vied for the opportunity to be considered a major league town to satisfy the needs to fill the new league. Major League Baseball, not wanting this challenge on their doorsteps, claimed that three of the prospective cities would conflict in territories that already represented in MLB, thus, aborting the Continental League's attempt a creating another major league. MLB then contracted four of the top cities, New York, Los Angeles, Washington, and Minneapolis-St. Paul, to be incorporated into the major leagues. (3)

The New York Yankees won the American League pennant five consecutive years, 1960–1964, and, winning the World Series in 1961 and 1962. However, their stars started to show their age and injuries and a lack of talent from the farm system caused the team to experience a steep drop in the standings after the 1964 season. The game also experienced seismic changes in the mid-sixties, beginning during the 1964 season. On August 14, 1964, William N. Wallace reported in *The New York Times*, "The Columbia Broadcasting System has purchased an 80% interest in the New York Yankees baseball organization from Daniel R, Topping and Del E. Webb. Mr. Topping and Mr. Webb retained 20% of the stock." The price paid by CBS totaled $14 million, with $11.2 million when consummated. (4) Wallace added, "The acquisition of a major sports power? by a major broadcasting "power" was confirmed yesterday by Joe Cronin, the president of the American League." (5) Michael Burke, CBS vice president, highly decorated World War II veteran, recipient of the Navy Cross and the Silver Star, and a former agent of OSS, (the Office of Strategic Services, the precursor to the CIA), was the point person in the purchase of the Yankees for CBS.

CBS's image did not look good at a time when rumors abounded that a communications operation threatened to take over the American League as they were in the process of negotiating the deal with the Yankees. To compound this negative conception, Yankee's favorite manager, Yogi Berra, was replaced, ironically, by the former St. Louis Cardinal's manager, Johnny Keane, who helped beat the Yankees in the 1964 World Series, only to be replaced by Ralph Houk eighteen months later. (6)

Another significant change in baseball's structure was the draft. As reported by Matt Kelly of the Baseball Hall of Fame, "Created in 1965 to restore competitive balance and to curb the inflated signing bonuses given to unproven players, the amateur draft is now recognized by MLB teams as a crucial tool to ensuring their long-term success." (7) The amateur draft offers the lower-ranked baseball teams the earliest selections to sign the best prospects from the talent pool. In effect, this hurt teams like the more successful Yankees and Dodgers who would, in most cases, be the preferred choice of the ballplayer.

Marvin Miller and the Players Union

For nearly a century after the baseball owners established the reserve clause, the players never obtained the critical legal services necessary to challenge the owners' provision. By late 1965, recognizing a need for more comprehensive representation, the Executive Board of the Major League Baseball Players Association (MLBPA), nominated a most learned man in labor-management relations, Marvin Miller, as their Executive Officer. He officially assumed his position in July 1966. His job was to do battle with the owners on the reserve clause. (8) Miller had an esteemed labor-management history. He graduated from NYU with an economics degree in 1938 and then he worked for:

- the National Labor Relations Board involving labor disputes
- the International Association of Machinists
- the United Auto Workers
- the United Steelworkers in1950 in becoming the union's chief economist (9)

The first issue that arose was that the players' minimum salary in 1947 was $5,000 and only $1,000 more in 1965, which led to the first collective bargaining agreement (CBA) in 1968. (10)

On February 21, 1968, The MLBPA history records: "The players and clubs agree to a first-ever Collective Bargaining Agreement, CBA-1, covering two years, effective January 1, 1968. It includes a minimum salary increase to $10,000; an improved and standardized contract form; increases in cash allowances for incidentals such as meals and spring training; a formalized procedure for grievances (to be heard by the commissioner); and new scheduling rules." (11)

Then, in November, Miller struck a deal with Topps, the manufacturer of baseball cards that became a significant part of the collectible era. It doubled the annual stipend to $250 per player, plus Topps would pay a royalty of 8% on revenue up to $4 million in sales, 10% after that. The players collected $320,000 in royalties in the first year of the deal. (12) After coming on board, Miller spearheaded players' grievances, salary disputes, pensions, and other situations of litigious nature. His positive effect was apparent. In 1969, Miller played a huge part in a watershed moment involvingthe contract of Curt Flood, who was a star ballplayer with the St. Louis Cardinals for twelve years. Flood was not happy with being traded to the Philadelphia Phillies in October of 1969. After seeking Marvin Miller's advice, he decided to reject the contract and sued baseball.

Curt Flood

The first issue that immediately drew Miller's attention was the fact that the players' minimum wage salary had "jumped" from $5,000 to only $6,000 in a period of inflation. After Miller engineered the first collective bargaining agreement between the players and owners in 1967 what loomed more significant in his mind was the reserve clause. This matter surfaced in 1969 with the landmark case of former St. Louis Cardinals' outfielder Curt Flood and how it set the tone for free agency. He was traded to the Philadelphia Phillies in 1969 after a great career with the Cardinals. Flood refused to go to Philadelphia to report to the Phillies, thus challenging the reserve clause. Flood, who had become deeply tied into the St. Louis community rejected the move to Philadelphia and sat out the entire season. He filed a lawsuit against Baseball Commissioner Bowie Kuhn, questioning the legality of the reserve clause. Flood strongly felt that he should be allowed to negotiate freely with other teams. The Supreme Court ultimately ruled against him in 1972. (13)

Men on the Moon and the Mets Win It All

Nineteen sixty-nine brought man's first walk on the moon and the first World Series championship to the New York Mets. The underdog Mets were the top team in the national pastime after beating the heavily favored Baltimore Orioles in an exciting World Series. The victory completed the flip in New York City baseball as the Yankees now suffered from mediocrity, at best. It produced an outbreak of partying for the New York Mets' baseball fans, including a ticker-tape parade up Broadway. To some, this feat paralleled the first human beings, Neil Armstrong and Buzz Aldrin, walking on the moon that same year. "One small step for man, one giant leap for mankind."

Major League Baseball continued to celebrate with the 100th anniversary of professional baseball, honoring the first professional touring baseball team, the Cincinnati Red Stockings. Major League Baseball and the Major League Baseball Players Association announced a joint donation of $1 million to the **Negro Leagues Baseball Museum** on the 100th anniversary of the creation of the Negro Leagues. (14) This decade indeed came to close in a flourish!

Joe DiMaggio, visiting the troops in Vietnam in 1969
Courtesy - Hall of Fame

CHAPTER 14

The Turbulent 1970s

a. Upheaval

b. Changing of the Guard

c. Massive Renovation and Collectables

d. Free Agency

e. The Bronx Zoo

f. Tragedy and Peace

Upheaval

The 1970s was a decade of upheaval and change almost everywhere in the country, but particularly in New York City. It all started with the US postal strike in New York City in 1970. Then in 1971, the New York City Police Department experienced cutbacks. Major League Baseball went on strike in 1972. The Twin Towers of the World Trade Center became the world's tallest buildings. The American "police action" in Vietnam ended, and an era of urban decay began. The country experienced a major fiscal crisis in 1975, hitting New York City especially hard. *The Daily News* illustrated President Ford's alleged reaction to NYC: "Drop Dead," the personal computer arrived, and then came a blackout of the entire city's electrical power grid in the heat of the summer while the "Son of Sam" terrorized the city in 1977. Arson in the Bronx was shown four times in the nationwide telecast during Game 2 of the World Series, which gave rise to the infamous statement, "The Bronx is burning." The newspaper strikes in 1978 shut down *The New York Times*, *The Daily News*, and *The New York Post* for two to three months, which hurt the New York teams considerably. This image stigmatized the Bronx for decades to come. All of this occurred to the strains of "disco fever" emanating from the Studio 54 nightclub. I had the "good" fortune of witnessing it all. By then Yankee Stadium was well on the way to becoming the "place to be" for major outdoor events in the country.

Baseball was also going through its struggles during this time. Through the course of the game's economic history, dark moments when the owners and the players did not see eye-to-eye resulted in either strikes or lockouts. In the first century of professional baseball, strikes threatened, some having nothing to do with financial matters. Major League Baseball Players Association with Marvin Miller as the executive director conducted the first significant strike from April 1 through April 13, 1972. Eighty-six irreplaceable games were lost as the season shortened. This work stoppage revolved around the players seeking compensation for the cost of living to be replaced by the owners' contributions to increase the players' pension plan. Although there was no clear winner, the owners satisfied most of the players' demands. (1)

In industrial stoppages as well as baseball work stoppages, strikes are initiated by employees and players, while the owners foster lock-outs. On the heels of the 1972 players' strike, the owners noted the absence of a collective bargaining agreement. They locked-out the players, preventing them from going to spring training. This stoppage lasted about two weeks until the two parties agreed on a three-year deal that introduced salary arbitration. (2) At this time, the owners began to realize the strength of the ballplayers' union, and they tried to prevent further losses in court.

Changing of the Guard

In the early 1970s, five decades of wear and tear on the "House that Ruth Built," were taking a heavy toll on the grand dame's superstructure. To add to the ballpark's general wear and tear, during a 'bat day' promotion, the fans tried to incite a rally by banging their bats on the stadium's concrete floor. "The pounding of the bats resulted in chunks of concrete falling. No one was hurt," stated by Marty Appel. (3) Safety had become an issue, and the only remedy that came out of it was to build a new ballpark.

Yankee Village, the neighborhood surrounding Yankee Stadium, had been in decline since the 1960s. "The realistic truth is that people will not go there anymore because it is not a nice place to go," claimed Dick Young of the New York *Daily News*. If it were not for Mayor John Lindsay, the 1970s might have been the final decade of the Yankees in the Bronx. There were other sites proposed for a new stadium. New Jersey lured the New York Giants football club away from the Stadium to the Meadowlands, where a new home for them opened in 1976. However, Mayor Lindsay, not wanting to lose the Yankees on his watch, struck a deal for New York City to perform a major renovation on Yankee Stadium. It would cost around $24 million and require the team and the offices to relocate temporarily to Shea Stadium, home of the New York Mets, for two years. (4) New neighborhood residents, Latino and Black, assimilated into the popular culture through baseball and Yankee Stadium was their home plate. A significant player in the renovation deal was the newly minted owner of the Yankees, George M. Steinbrenner III. As Sam Roberts of *The New York Times* reported, "Mr. Arthur R. Taylor, president of CBS, unloaded the New York Yankees in 1973. He oversaw the sale of CBS's share of the Yankees to a group of investors led by Mr. Steinbrenner for $10 million. CBS had purchased 80 percent of the team for $11.2 million in 1964." (5)

In 1966, the Yankees finished last in the American League for the first time since 1912. The team struggled, rarely ranking higher than fourth by the time CBS sold its share; then, they finished in second place in 1972. Michael Burke, promised the president's role to stay on with the team, was not appreciative of the not-so buttoned-up appearance of Mr. Steinbrenner, putting Burke on a slippery slope to his ouster. Burke was gone by April 1973. By the end of the year, manager Ralph Houk and general manager Lee MacPhail had also departed.

In this turbulent era, two Yankees players caught widespread attention as Fritz Peterson, and Mike Kekich swapped families. The two left-handed starting pitchers were close friends and roommates on the road, and the men became enamored with each other's wives. The subject of changing partners came up late in 1972 during a party at the newspaper's writer Maury Allen's home in New Jersey. Six months later, the deal consummated as the two pitchers exchanged lives, kids, houses, and all, with each man moving into the other's family home. The renovation of the Stadium loomed. (6)

Massive Renovation/Collectibles

What fans referred to as the Stadium's "aura and mystique"—the lingering light of the great ballplayers, the great personalities, and the significant events held here—would end for good on September 30, 1973, with the final game of the season. The closing of the Stadium's doors opened another door in our pop culture: collectibles. Everybody wanted a piece of this historic edifice!

Yankees' president, Gabe Paul, offered a token of appreciation to the approximately 6,000 season ticket holders by giving them actual Stadium seats as a token of appreciation for their loyalty. The Invirex Demolition Company removed them. Only around 4,000 ticketholders' seats were accounted for. The rest were on put on sale to the public. A department store, E.J. Korvette, managed to get a boatload of the chairs and sold them at $7 each. (7) A few hundred also made their way to War Memorial Stadium, a Minor League ballpark in Greensboro, North Carolina.

With reconstruction completed, the Yankees returned to their newly refurbished Stadium in 1976. The significant renovations included a cantilevered support system holding up the tiers. The 106 cables required for support surrounded the Stadium, replacing the obstructive girders that supported the mezzanine and upper level. The hard-wooden seats were replaced with softer plastic seats. A new mercury-vapor lighting system replaced the banks of incandescent lights installed in 1946. Unfortunately, there was to be no spring training as the disgruntled Major League Baseball owners approved a lockout.

Free Agency/Revenue Sharing

Despite daily brush fires with Mr. Steinbrenner, a.k.a. "The Boss," Billy Martin, and Reggie Jackson, the Yankees won the pennant by once again beating Kansas City, then besting the Dodgers in six games in the 1977 World Series. In the clincher, Reggie Jackson, who signed as a free agent in 1976, electrified the Stadium crowd and the national television viewers by hitting three home runs on three consecutive pitches off three different pitchers, a feat never before accomplished in World Series play. Jackson won Most Valuable Player honors for the Series. The victory was followed by a ticker-tape parade up the "Canyon of Heroes" (Broadway), which was thrilling for me as a participant. The drama did not end there.

Another significant disruption of the decade was the introduction of free agency to Major League Baseball. On New Year's Eve of 1974, New York Yankees President, Gabe Paul, signed ace Oakland A's pitcher Jim "Catfish" Hunter. Oakland A's owner, Charles O. Finley, reneged on a $50,000 insurance policy that he owed Hunter, and Hunter took the case to court. MLBPA executive Marvin Miller challenged the reserve clause in a contentious hearing. Peter Seitz, the official arbitrator, ruled in a landmark decision declaring that Hunter would become the first free agent. On December 24, 1975, the first actual test of the strength of the newly emplaced free agency rule came about through the dual cases of pitchers David McNally and Andy Messersmith. They declared that their contracts no longer bound them and that they could now sell their services to the highest bidder. It was an iconic moment in baseball history and, finally, the death knell of the reserve clause. (9)

The face of the game had also changed with the controversial 1973 adoption of the "Designated Hitter" rule by the American League. With this rule, the pitcher was replaced in the batting order by a legitimate batter, as the hitting was not a strong suit of the pitcher. A more exciting offense was then instantly created as a result.

In one case of appreciation for Stadium memorabilia, collector-author Bert Sugar signed two checks, each for $1,500, payable to the New York Yankees to appropriate some of the artifacts that were left behind. In a short time, some of the removed artifacts, including the chairs, were selling for thousands of dollars. Sugar said, "I put two kids through college and had plenty left over." (8)

One of the most exciting comebacks in baseball history came about in 1978 involving the Boston Red Sox and the New York Yankees. Coming off a 1977 World Series victory, the Yankees were a distant 14 ½ games behind the Red Sox in June. But the Red Sox started to tail off in the standings as the Yankees mounted a comeback. By early September, the gap was down to four games with a four-game series at Fenway Park on the slate. In what came to be known as "The Boston Massacre," the Yankees swept all four games, outscoring the Red Sox 42–9. By season's end, both teams were tied in the standings, prompting a dramatic one-game playoff at Fenway Park. Many people call the Boston Red Sox/New York Yankees the "greatest rivalry in professional sports" because of moments like this one: light-hitting Yankees' shortstop Bucky Dent hit a three-run homer in the seventh inning to put the Yankees on top, eventually winning the game. They went on to beat the Kansas City Royals in the American League Championship Series to enter the World Series. The Yankees then beat the Dodgers again in six games to win the World Series.

The Bronx Zoo

Yankees reliever Sparky Lyle had been instrumental in the Yankees' success in 1977, capped off with the Cy Young award. Lyle was the first American League relief pitcher to achieve that distinction. The month after the parade, Steinbrenner picked up the hottest reliever on the free-agent market in Goose Gossage—providing the team with an embarrassment of riches and a crushing blow to Lyle. Lyle would spend a season playing an unhappy second fiddle to Goose and then was traded to Texas. Lyle's unhappy '78 season was fuel to the fire of his book, *The Bronx Zoo*, co-authored by Peter Golenbock. "The name of the book came to characterize the whole late '70s era of Yankee baseball when the team achieved success despite mountains of controversy," stated Marty Appel in his *Pinstripe Empire*. (10) Another significant loss occurred. The architect of the Yankees' success, Gabe Paul, resigned after the 1977 season and departed for Cleveland. Steinbrenner claimed Paul was getting too much of the credit for the player moves and the team's success.

Across town, the Mets showed that they were not immune to drama either. The greatest ballplayer in the Mets' young fifteen-year history—pitcher Tom Seaver, who was called "The Franchise" by the Mets' chairman of the board, M. Donald Grant—become embroiled in a contract dispute. Grant felt that Seaver's demand for a salary of $250,000 was nothing but greed. Seaver, traded to Cincinnati for four nondescript ballplayers, broke Mets fans' hearts.

Tragedy and Peace

In 1979 with the turbulent decade drawing to a close, the Yankees lingered around fourth place for most of the season. Alas, another comeback was not in the making. However, none could predict the tragedy that would strike. Thurman Munson's career as a catcher was winding down by 1979, and injuries had taken their toll (11) though Munson had never spent a day on the disabled list. When a plane crash claimed his life on August 2, 1979, it closed a chapter on the Yankees' decade.

Following is an interview with schoolteacher, fan, and season ticketholder, Ms. Joan Gianmarino, on how baseball connected to her:

> **Thurman Munson was the first ballplayer that connected me to the game of baseball and the Yankees. Besides his skills as a player, the toughness with which he played the game, and his personality drew me in as a young girl just starting to learn and love the game. He was a great presence for me on the team that I can barely put into words. Thurman certainly had his unique way of playing the game. No other player had ever affected me the way he did when I watched him play. After 40 plus years, I still cry, get nostalgic, and feel like a brand-new fan again whenever his name appears, or I see a video or picture of him. Thurman had everything to do with me being the Yankees season-ticket holder I have been for the last 47 years.(12)**

Years later, his image still invokes grit and determination at a time when leadership was on display daily as he pushed his teammates toward glory. Munson's story was a vignette of authentic leadership and character. It fitted that peace came to Yankee Stadium on October 2, 1979. In a venerable mass said by Pope John Paul ll, with over 80,000 faithful followers, this grand event wrapped up the raucous decade.

On Veterans Day, one month later, I conducted the first formal tour of Yankee Stadium at the behest of the Bronx County Historical Society. A few years later, we opened the tours to the public, and they have since become an integral part of the Yankees' organization with the revenue benefitting the Yankee Foundation, a non-profit 501-c-3 program. The revenue benefits the educational and recreational programs for inner-city youth. The Stadium tours have now been running for 40 years. To speak of the popularity of Yankee Stadium, we can take the Year of 2008 for example, the last year in the old Stadium before moving to a new ballpark across 161st Street. That year over 150,000 tourists visited the Stadium—many of whom did not speak English, attesting to the global popularity of this mecca. At that time, we also introduced a special tour for the Wounded Warrior Project and the Special Operations Warrior Foundation to acknowledge those who paid the price for our freedom.

In retrospect of the '70s, two great personalities arose that have an effect on the game until this time... Marvin Miller, who helped elevate the stature of the ballplayer as a result of the reserve clause and George Steinbrenner, who helped his powerhouse team establish the first of two dynasties with his "winning" attitude transcending the entire organization. Marvin Miller gained entry into the Hall of Fame after being voted in 2019. George Steinbrenner still garners support for Hall of Fame status.

Marvin Miller
Courtesy - Hall of Fame

George M. Steinbrenner
Courtesy - Hall of Fame

CHAPTER 15

The 1980s-A Decade of Transition

> **a. 1981 Work Stoppage**
> **b. Parity**
> **c. 1985 Strike**
> **d. Earthquake during the '89 World Series**

1981 Work Stoppage

The first summer that the national pastime took from the people was in 1981. Soon after the Collective Bargaining Agreement expired at the end of 1979, the owners were seeking compensation for the loss of free agents. The players and owners discussed the situation and reached an agreement in principle. The stumbling block was whether to allow the free agency issue considered during the season. Following an eight-day players' strike toward the end of spring training, a preliminary four-year agreement was tendered before the players' potential May 23 strike date.

The agreement, in principle, allowed the issue of free agency to be reopened the following season. However, with no deal in sight, the players went on strike on June 12, 1981. It lasted for 50 days. Hard to imagine summer without baseball. But, when the owners' strike insurance was about to expire, a settlement was reached on July 31 that instituted a new rule for 'loss of player' compensation. A total of 712 games were lost due to the strike. (1)

In his book *A Whole Different Ball Game: The Sport and Business of Baseball*, Marvin Miller drew the financial resolution to the strike:

> **Salary losses for the players during the strike averaged about $52,000 and totaled almost 34 million dollars, a fraction of the loss the owners had intended to inflict on them by stifling free agency. The players successful resistance led to a phenomenal growth of their salaries, starting the very next year. The average prestrike salary of almost $186,000 increased by $56,000 in 1982; by 1985 it had doubled to $371,000, and by 1990 it had more than tripled to over $597,000. The player payroll of less than $121 million dollars in 1981 exceeded $388 million in 1990. (2)**

Collateral damage was done, though, as many season ticket holders who patronized the restaurants in Yankee Stadium before the strike, were not to be found after play resumed.

Parity—Finally

As a result of the strike, many disappointed fans pursued other forms of entertainment. Once baseball returned, not all of those season ticketholders returned to the ballpark. Free agency also caused changes in the game. From 1980 to 1992, only the Dodgers and Twins won two World Series, and every other World Series victor, including the 1986 Mets, was a different team. Five of them were from smaller markets. A total of nine teams won World Series in the 1980s. Free agency regenerated the fans' excitement in their favorite teams, which produced a marked increase in attendance.

Many claimed that baseball in the '80s had become a forgotten era, basically because of the lack of offense and the emergence of the pitcher's relief role as the "closer," whose specific purpose was to record the final out. Dan D'Addona wrote:

> **"The lack of power is just one of the many reasons the 1980s remains an overlooked era. Few things are celebrated from the 1980s, and much of what is remembered is negative: the 1981 strike, a cocaine scandal, umpire Don Denkinger's blown call in the 1985 World Series, the banishment of all-time hits leader Pete Rose for gambling, an earthquake postponing the 1989 World Series, and the spread of Astroturf." (3)**

1985 Strike

In 1985, the players struck again. Armed with bad legal advice (reportedly from the commissioner), the owners thought that salary arbitration would hold down salaries. However, the players' salaries skyrocketed contrary to the thoughts of the owners, who felt that they would be able to adjust the agreement. The players flatly turned down the owners' requests. In just two days the owners, realizing that this was a losing cause, conceded, and the short-lived strike ended.

The winter of 1985-1986 had such an empty feeling, especially in the "hot stove league." This term arose from the time when the die-hard baseball fans supposedly gathered around a pot-bellied stove and spoke of nothing but baseball. In that winter, they discussed trades, rule changes, the health of the game, and free agency. Strangely, there were in the dead of winter no big signings by any of the 29 prospective free agents who were looking for increased salaries when the free agency period opened. The owners' subterfuge continued for the next few years, oddly with the support of a new baseball commissioner, Peter Ueberroth. An arbitrator ruled that the owners had conspired in violation of the CBA (Collective Bargaining Agreement) that prohibited such action and awarded the players damages. Three arbitration rulings found the owners guilty of collusion and assessed costs of nearly $300 million in the first phase of damage payments. (4)

Meanwhile, the raucous New York Mets won their second World Series in 1986. After the Mets were outs away on the brink of losing the Series, a fatal error by the Red Sox first baseman breathed new life into the moribund team as they began to snatch victory out of the jaws of defeat. The Mets won that game and eventually won Game 7 of the World Series for the championship.

Ueberroth retired in disgrace a year before his contract was to expire. Former Yale president, A. Bartlett Giamatti, succeeded Ueberroth as the commissioner of Major League Baseball on April 1, 1989, after more than two years as president of the National League. On September 1, five months to the day later, Giamatti succumbed to a heart attack, and he died at the age of 51.

Giamatti is best known for taking on Pete Rose, the hard-nosed Cincinnati Reds manager and former playing star. Rose was accused of having a secret passion for gambling, including betting on his team. Rose had little choice and consented to his ban from baseball in a written agreement while still denying that he bet on his own team's games. (5) He later acknowledged that he did. Rose, the hustling star, still holds the major league baseball record for all-time hits.

As reported by Robert McFadden, *The New York Times*, "A. Bartlett Giamatti, the Renaissance scholar and former president of Yale University who gave up a brilliant academic career in 1986 to join the rough-and-tumble of big-league baseball, suffered a heart attack and passed away at his summer home." (6) Following is an essay by the great scholar and philosopher from in his book, *A Great and Glorious Game: Baseball Writings of A. Bartlett Giamatti by A. Bartlett Giamatti et al.*:

The Green Fields of the Mind

It breaks your heart. It is designed to break your heart. The game begins in the spring, when everything else begins again,

and it blossoms in the summer, filling the afternoons and eve-
nings, and then as soon as the chill rains come, it stops and
leaves you to face the fall alone. You count on it, rely on it to
buffer the passage of time, to keep the memory of sunshine
and high skies alive, and then just when the days are all twi-
light, when you need it most, it stops. Today, October 2, a
Sunday of rain and broken branches and leaf-clogged drains
and slick streets, it stopped, and summer was gone. (7)

Earthquake during the '89 World Series

On October 17, 1989, an earthquake measuring 7.1 on the Richter
scale struck Loma Prieta in northern California, killing 67 people and
causing $7 billion worth of damage. The tragedy struck less than half
an hour before Game 3 of the World Series between the Oakland A's
and the San Francisco Giants at San Francisco's Candlestick Park. Ten
days later, play resumed as the A's swept the Giants in the Series four
games to none. This was the first earthquake in the United States to be
nationally televised. (8)

CHAPTER 16

The 1990s: A Decade of Two Dynasties

a. Strike and Prosperity
b. The Lost Season
c. How PEDs Saved Baseball
d. New Stadia Explosion

Strikes and Prosperity

From 1975 through 1979, baseball operated by two perspectives, as a result of the reserve clause, ownership, and the ballplayers, But, in the nearly half-century since free agency evolved, the push and pull of the two agencies have become much more enjoined to the business of baseball as a result of strikes and lockouts. While the owners garnered substantial rewards, the players also profited. The price of a ticket continually escalated, as did the concessions and parking. The game's revenue became the focal point at this time, all of which had a positive impact on the country's growing economy.

However, checks and balances were still the order of the day. So, as this decade opened in 1990, the owners who had not received the message that the players had their business act together, attempted a salary cap and revenue sharing as free agency was growing steadily. The players rejected the owners' proposition, virtually canceling spring training. The full regular-season games, in fact, did remain intact.

A Lost Season

Another work stoppage emerged as the players flatly refused the owners' demands in 1994. The owners wanted to eliminate arbitration. In a short time, and with the Collective Bargaining Agreement about to expire in December, the players struck on August 12 in the belief that the owners would continue to give in. This time the owners stood firm, and the players went on strike. From observation by noted columnist George F. Will:

> **Both owners and players are broadly disdained by fans increasingly disinclined to regard baseball as oxygen— essential. But fans, at first marginally partial to the owners' side, increasingly understand that the owners, or a controlling cabal of them, are the aggressors, demanding large changes in the status quo of baseball's compensation system and that the players struck defensively to avoid unilateral imposition of changes by ownership.(1)**

By September, when there was no movement as both sides drew their lines, Major League Baseball canceled all postseason play, including baseball's nationwide attraction, the World Series. It was the first time since 1904 that there was no World Series. The strike lasted 232 days, and the 1995 season shortened to 144 games. In a stunning rebuke of the owner's demands and after only 15 minutes of testimony, Judge Sonia Sotomayor ended the strike, ruling against the owners by issuing an injunction against the owners for alleged violations of the National Labor Relations Act and ordering that they comply with the expired Collective Bargaining Agreement. In 2009, sports enthusiast, President Barack

Obama stated, "Some say that Judge Sotomayor saved baseball." Judge Sotomayor said, "You can't grow up in the South Bronx without knowing baseball." (2) Many fans unhappy with the recent events, or non-events in this case, subsequently did not return to the game precipitating a 20 percent drop in attendance.

While the 1980s were symbolic of parity among the teams, only two teams dominated the 1990s. The Atlanta Braves made it to the post-season eight times winning one World Series victory, and the New York Yankees won four World Series in 1996, 1998, 1999, and 2000, Ironically, the Yankees' success was not achieved entirely through free agency but by savvy trades and their farm system.

How PEDs Saved Baseball

Fans that became disillusioned with the game after the strike and walked away from baseball started to return to the game as baseball, once again, showed its resiliency. The Performance Enhancing Drug/Steroid, (PED/Steroid) era brought back many of the worn-out strike fans in 1998 due to the mighty home run (which had saved the game in 1920), and perhaps due to weaker pitching, specifically the chase between two of the game's better-known sluggers, Mark McGuire and Sammy Sosa. The two sluggers dueled throughout the 1998 season to break Roger Maris's 61 home run record set in 1961, thrilling the fans. Gorn and Goldstein offered in *A Brief History of American Sports*, "Maybe because of baseball's storied past as our [national pastime], Congress got involved in the scandal, calling hearings and inviting some of the biggest stars to testify."(3)

The expansion also increased the home run totals as the new teams had weaker pitching staffs, which increased the power surge. The upper echelon pitchers, protected from the talent pool, were offered to the new teams. In addition, the new tighter wound baseballs that traveled farther in the recently built smaller ballparks was a significant factor in the increased home run production. Older ballparks seeking to improve the offense moved their fences in. Furthermore, the training regimens, including better nutrition and better training facilities, enhanced players' skills as the players became more prominent and more durable.

In 1999, Barry Bonds was upset with the San Francisco Giants' management over a contract dispute. He arrived at the camp after he had put on fifteen pounds of rock-hard muscle in fifteen days and an increase in hat size. His teammates referred to him as "The Incredible Hulk." When Bonds took batting practice, he drove the ball farther than ever. To teammates, writers, and fans in Scottsdale, Arizona, and especially to Giants management, Bonds' appearance and performance raised a fundamental question of "what in the hell had he been doing in the offseason," said Lance Williams and Mark Fainaru-Wada in their book *Game of Shadows*. (4)

Although the use of performance-enhancing drugs had reportedly been around since the 1980s, it was at this time that there appeared to be a tremendous increase in player usage PEDs. Without a doubt, player records achieved during this era will have some type of notification, perhaps an asterisk, that they set during the PED era, a period that tarnished our national pastime.

In *Faith and Freedom*, Andrew Harvey said:

The factors and the magic that comprise the game of baseball are why baseball survived the Black Sox scandal, overcame racism and integrated on its own without government intervention, persevered despite the advent of the designated hitter, and will outlast the consequences of the steroid era. In its complicities, tolerations, repudiations, and expiations, baseball has mirrored both America's vices and virtues. The histories of baseball and America are entwined forever. (5)

The Team of the Century

Significant events that perpetuated throughout the 1998 season was the New York Yankees' pursuit of the all-time wins in a season, which was set by the Chicago Cubs when they won 116 games in 1906. Although the Yankees fell two wins short of that mark, they did establish a Major League record, winning eleven postseason victories, including the World Series, totaling 125 victories. Many have called this version of the New York Yankees, the best team in baseball history. They went on to win the 1998 World Series and then justifiably came to be called by many, "The Team of the Century" after winning it all again in 1999.

PART THREE

CHAPTER 17

The Twenty-first Century

a. Television

b. Yankees and Mets

c. September 11, 2001

d. Sabermetrics

e. The Mitchell Report

f. The Closing of Yankee Stadium

Television

Asignificant change in the broadcast production of baseball games began in the mid-1990s with television's importance to the game through the revenue it generated mainly by way of cable networking. The prestige that it had garnered for cable did not go unnoticed. Leonard Koppett, in his *Concise History of Major League Baseball,* may have said it best:

> Sports programming fills many hours while costing much less to produce than other types of programs like sitcoms or movies. With the proliferation of hundreds of channels and

24 hours to fill every day, sports were more necessary than ever. In addition, sports present an unparalleled opportunity for advertisers to reach a particular audience, representing an attractive demographic to whom products and other programs can be sold. (1)

In a statement from Rick Cerrone, Editor-in-Chief, *Baseball Digest,* Cerrone touches on the progression of the media from its earliest stages of development to the present:

In the early days of baseball, the media--all print all of the time--was the primary means of promoting the game. It delivered everything from the season's schedule to game results with ball clubs having little, if any, other ways to reach their fans. Other platforms joined in over the 20th century. First radio and later television. And both pro-vided promotional opportunities as well as challenges for teams. Will broadcasting or televising home games nega-tively impact attendance? This was a much-debated issue for many years.

The impact of the print media remained significant for much, if not all, of the last century. Even as the number of dailies covering Major League Baseball in New York alone dropped from dozens to a handful, they still drove fan interest daily. Even with TV and radio available, a newspaper strike in the seventies was considered disastrous for New York baseball teams. That would not be the case today.

As we entered the 21st century, the impact of newspaper coverage began to change as ball clubs now had the ability--with their regional networks and digital platforms--to promote their product. While George Steinbrenner always measured the

popularity of his teams by the number of back pages in the New York tabloids they merited, that is likely no longer the case.

Newspapers and their digital platforms, especially in New York, still play a role, but it's different today with entire networks now devoted to each team. With their news reporting, they still wield significant power but not the ability to drive fans to the ballpark as they once did. (2)

One can easily envision the transfer of power in a televised production of baseball games, leaning more toward the big money of cable. So, as baseball had been struggling with the loyalty of fans, Major League Baseball had to acquiesce to the demands of the networks. This created the problem of starting times of the games, compounded by extended game lengths, and many intrusive commercials. How can a youngster, the target market for the games, be able to enjoy a game that runs well into the night? Most post-season games start at 8:37 p.m. Eastern Time, nearer the youngster's bedtime.

When the Yankees' $494 million-dollar twelve-year agreement with the Madison Square Garden Network of televised games expired, the Yankees launched their own YES (Yankee Entertainment and Sports) network in 2002. Koppett wrote:

Convinced that their telecasts were worth even more than cable outlets were willing to pay, they decided to create their channel and charge fees directly to cable operators. The result was messy. Some cable companies refused to pay, leaving millions of irate New Yorkers unable to watch the Bronx Bombers. However, officials of other teams followed the Yankees lead, seduced by similar math. (3)

Yankees and Mets

New York City once again became the epicenter of baseball in 2000. In August, a fever started to grip the city with the thought of a possible confrontation between the two New York teams meeting in the World Series in October. The fans began to show their support by wearing their team's colors all over town. Banter and prayers were heard in coffee shops, delis, restaurants, and on the street corners of the Big Apple. The penant-winning game, after a dramatic home run by Yankee David Justice, Yankees' broadcaster Michael Kay cried, "Get your tokens ready, you might be boarding the subway." The Yankees did take the World Series 4 games to 1 over the Mets.

September 11, 2001

On September 10, 2001, the New York Yankees recognized the efforts of the Bronx Little League team that had just won the Little League World Series in Williamsport, Pennsylvania. I was asked to acknowledge their efforts on behalf of the New York Yankees to a large crowd showing their Bronx pride on the steps of the Bronx County Building, just a few blocks from Yankee Stadium. The young players on a flatbed truck traveled through the neighborhood to the delight of the crowd. Unfortunately, it was later discovered that their star pitcher was a 15-year-old ringer, above the Little League age limit. Thus, the team was disqualified from the trophy and the title.

The next day four 767 Boeing passenger planes fully loaded with jet fuel brought to the world a devastating tragedy. Two of the planes hit New York's Twin Towers, one hit the Pentagon in Washington, D.C., and the fourth plane, headed for Washington, D.C., was hijacked by four bomb-toting terrorists. The terrorists rerouted the plane, supposedly to hit the Capitol or the White House, but a handful of passengers turned into heroes. One of the heroes on Flight 93 was Todd Beamer. After a soul-searching, prayerful few minutes, he said to his fellow heroes, "Are you ready? Okay. 'Let's roll!'" which was overheard by a telephone operator, and the rescue attempt began. This action caused a major disruption in the terrorists' plans as the plane went into a free-fall and crashed into a field in Shanksville, Pennsylvania, killing all on board. (4) Lisa Beamer and her two children were guests of the Yankees during the 2001 World Series. I met Lisa and her two youngsters a month after the tragedy in Yankee Stadium. As I approached her, I received a warm greeting with a great smile!

Then-president, George W. Bush, preparing to throw out the ceremonial first pitch before Game Three of the 2001 World Series. 10/30/2001
Courtesy - Library of Congress

Once again, baseball was a way to help to heal the country. With the games suspended for ten days, the national pastime took on a whole new meaning when play resumed on September 21st at Shea Stadium with the New York Mets hosting their bitter rivals, the Atlanta Braves. In the pre-game ceremonies, with smoke still coming out of Ground Zero, one instantly saw how the two teams came together by shaking hands in an expression of unity, unlike any other time on the baseball diamond. This form of togetherness resonated throughout the country. Emotions were not only running high at the ballpark but all over the land. With patriotism already excited in the crowd, Mets' catcher, Mike Piazza, hit a dramatic home run to put the Mets in the lead for good. Baseball was back. Piazza later stated, "I'm glad I could give people a diversion from the sorrow, to give them a thrill." Ultimately, it was a wonderful process of healing, not only for New York but for the country. Well said, Mike!

A month later, following the Arizona Diamondbacks' victories in the first two World Series games held in Phoenix, Arizona, the Series returned to New York. President George W. Bush threw out the ceremonial first pitch, which was never done by a sitting president during the World Series. As he strode out to the mound from the Yankees' dugout in a New York Fire Department pullover, the president was greeted by thunderous applause. After throwing a strike, he returned to the dugout, and the crowd of around 55,000 started to chant, "USA, USA." It was chilling! The New York Yankees went on to win Game 3. Once again, throughout the land, everybody was pulling for New York (except maybe in Phoenix).

With two remarkable comeback victories in Games 4 and 5, the Yankees snatched victory out of the jaws of defeat. In the bottom of the ninth inning, the Diamondbacks were leading with two outs and no one on base on each day. Yankees players had gone to witness the destruction at 'Ground Zero.' Inspired by what they had seen, they thrillingly won the next two back-to-back games. Many people across the country and around the globe who may not have necessarily been New York Yankees' fans were rooting for the Yankees in this heart-pounding World Series. However, when the Diamondbacks won the last two games in Arizona, the World Series ended abruptly. But for those three days, baseball in New York was at the epicenter of many peoples' hearts and minds as they were recovering in an all too fleeting moment from the cowardly attack on the Eleventh of September.

The Florida Marlins beat the Yankees in the 2003 World Series. It was their second championship since coming into the majors in 1993. Then, in the following year, the Boston Red Sox expunged the "Curse of the Babe" after 86 long and frustrating years in not winning the World

Series. They accomplished this feat in grand style as they came back from a 3-0 deficit in the American League Championship Series to defeat their nemesis, the New York Yankees, by taking four straight games from them in dramatic fashion. The Red Sox then went on to beat the St. Louis Cardinals in a four-game sweep of the World Series.

Sabermetrics

What contributed to the success of the Boston Red Sox winning four World Series championships from 2004–2018 was the growth of analytic assessment referred to as SABERMETRICS. Following is an excerpt of my interview with Mr. Nicholas Sette, MLB Data Quality Analyst:

Much like the game of baseball and the players on the field continue to change, the statistics themselves also go through evolutionary periods. With the basic rate and counting statistics leaving some fans unsatisfied, groups of passionate baseball enthusiasts decided to create new means of valuing performance. The family of statistics these passionate and highly educated fans created include acronyms such as WAR, Win Shares, DRS, and wOBA. The general baseball congregation viewed these statistical acronyms as hieroglyphics, and that one needed a Ph.D. to understand these numbers and how they came about.

Of all the advanced statistics that were born in the early 2000s, WAR, or Wins Above Replacement, would be the most contentious. Furthermore, as baseball analytics continued to grow in popularity, technology evolved to offer interesting and important data, not only to baseball operations staff but also to the fans. In 2015, MLB developed a brand-new way to appraise on-field performance through a system known as Statcast. This state-of-the-art tracking technology allows for the collection and analysis of a massive amount of baseball data.

Data Statcast provides a measurement in the velocity of how hard the ball was hit (Exit Velocity), the launch angle, and the spin-rate of the pitch in RPM. This extra information allows fans and executives alike to understand the play on the field at a much deeper level. And, as Statcast continues to grow, terms like Exit Velocity, Launch Angle, and Spin Rate are quickly becoming a part of the baseball fan's lexicon. These statistics are allowing fans to understand not only why a player is good but also what moves him to that level.

All of this most recent information has given executives another tool to use in their decision-making process. Moreover, a basic knowledge of the analytics mentioned above has also contributed to a high degree the fan's interest in the game. Whether at the ballpark or in their living-room, MLB, through Statcast, has given fans another way to enjoy our national pastime. (5)

The Mitchell Report

"The Mitchell Report," or "Report to the Commissioner of Baseball of an Independent Investigation into the Illegal Use of Steroids and Other Performance Enhancing Substances by Players in Major League Base-ball," culminated former US Senator George J. Mitchell's investigation into the use of steroids and human growth hormone (HGH) in Major League Baseball. (6) When the report finally came out in December 2007, it uncovered the history of illegal performance-enhancing sub-stances used by 89 players and the awakening that it had on the Major League Baseball drug testing program. The Bay Area Laboratory Co-Operative (BALCO) supplied the players with the venue for the drugs used by the players. With the findings of the Mitchell Report, the 2007 baseball season introduced the revised 2001 random testing for steroid policy, which enforced harsher penalties than ever before for steroid use in Major League Baseball. Several players were suspended under the new system. (7)

On December 4, 2003, the government's perjury case against Barry Bonds for lying to a grand jury, emerged in vivid detail. Over 200 pages of evidence became available. Pages included documents tying Bonds to four positive tests for steroids and calendars that prosecutors described as doping schedules. (8) Yet, Bonds was exonerated.

Meanwhile, the game of Baseball was going international. National teams competed in a series called the World Baseball Classic. Each team drew on the country's best available players. Finalists in the World Baseball Classic of 2006 were Japan, Cuba, Korea, and the Dominican Republic. The United States, with three wins and three losses, failed to qualify for the semi-finals. Japan won the Classic defeating Cuba in the single championship game. Korea at 6–1 had the best overall Classic record.

The Closing of Yankee Stadium

Yankee Stadium was not only an icon in America's popular culture, it was more than that. It was a state of mind while playing host to the incredible 26 New York Yankees World Series championship teams. During this time, names like Ruth, Gehrig, DiMaggio, Mantle, Jackson, Jeter, and Rivera, just to name a few, could roll off any fan's tongue without a stretch of the imagination. The names come to life in an exclusive area of Yankee Stadium called "Monument Park," where retired numbers, plaques, and, in exceptional cases, monuments attest to the exclusivity of these icons. There is no other like it in any sporting arena.

The wear and tear on this green cathedral rendered it beyond repair. Early in the 1998 season, a 500 pound expansion joint of concrete and steel loosened its moorings in the upper deck and fell onto the seats below in the Loge level. Fortunately, it was a few hours before game time, causing no harm to the ticketholder as ensuing inspections showed other potential problems. The repairs were forbidding. Mr. Steinbrenner, who had been campaigning for a new ballpark, now had sufficient evidence to explore the possibility and site for a new ballpark. On August 16, 2006, ground broke for the new Yankee Stadium.

September 21, 2008, marked the last day of this grand edifice. Many players of yesteryear were represented on the field at their respective positions in an elaborate pre-game ceremony. The greats who were not able to attend were represented by family members or, in some cases, by Yankees staff. Standing in a Yankees uniform serving Yankees' pitching ace, Allie Reynolds, from the "Golden Era" of New York City baseball, (1947-1957), was the thrill of a lifetime for me. What a great feeling it was listening to the cheers of the sellout crowd upon introduction while looking back over sixty years of my life and what part Yankees' baseball played in it.

A beautiful new Yankee Stadium opened in 2009 across the street from the original Stadium's site with more fan-friendly amenities, increased parking facilities, and 7,000 fewer seats, and the signature of Yankee Stadium, the frieze that adorned the fascia of the roof, was back in place. The cost came to $1.6 billion. The Yankees went on to christen the new building the same way that they had christened the original Stadium—with a World Series Championship.

CHAPTER 18

The Game

The Flow of the Game

One of the primary reasons for the flow of the game seemingly coming to a crawl is the use of specialized relief pitching. Complete games are now a rarity. The specialization of the relievers currently contributes significantly to the length of the game.

During post-season play, when most of the games on the east coast start between 8:07 and 8:37 p.m. with an average game time of three hours and 20 minutes, the viewers would be into the wee hours if they wished to catch the final out. Besides, postseason commercial breaks are more extended than regular-season breaks, further extending the game. Seventeen between-inning breaks (one after every half-inning except the final one), plus pitching change breaks (which are also longer in the postseason), adds around 17 minutes. This is baked into every postseason game. So, if you want to know what an average postseason game is, start at 3 hours, 20 minutes. (1) For example, in a recent game (Game 2) in the American League Championship Series, the starting time was 8:07 p.m.; the game did not end until 12:55 a.m.

Decisions, Decisions

Managerial decisions are evolving with the use of analytics. Managers refer to analytic data presented by the Baseball Operations Department, as stated earlier before any lineup card is presented. Other substitutions take place as the manager's role diminishes. Artificial Intelligence (AI) determines what the best lineup will be on the strength of the up-to-date performance of each player through the interpretation of analytics. However, there are factors that AI cannot determine, including the health and psychological presence as to a player's readiness to give 100%.

Hitters are on pace to slug more home runs than ever. However, they are also swinging and missing at record rates while seeing more pitches, drawing more walks, as pitchers are making way more relief appearances. (2) "Where it gets troubling, from a fan's perspective, is the number of strikeouts which are at an all-time high, no action, lots of specialty pitching changes," Baseball Commissioner Rob Manfred stated. "That combination is troubling to me."

In today's baseball climate, players are now reaching 40 and 50 home runs in a season. For example, Mets rookie Pete Alonzo led the Major Leagues by hitting 53 home runs in 2019, now a record for rookies. This feat assured him many votes toward his Rookie of the Year award. The emphasis on swinging for home runs by adjusting the launch angle of their swing has been accompanied by a general decline in hitting, causing batting averages to fall and strikeouts to reach all-time highs.

The Pitching Revolution

NY Times journalist Tyler Kepner offered this observation on August 16, 2018:

> **"This could be the first season in Major League history to feature more strikeouts than hits, a slowdown that worries many main League officials. 30 years ago, batters compiled nearly 13,000 more hits than strikeouts. Last season, that edge dwindled to about 2,000. This season it was nearly even with hits only slightly ahead: 30,678 hits to 30,569 strikeouts." (3)**

With the uptick in strikeouts, the strain placed on the pitcher's arm to fire baseballs at speeds upwards of 100 miles per hour has taken a toll along with snapping off curveballs with high torque. More and more arm surgeries are needed to correct the problem from the torque applied by the pitcher's arm. This process may shut down a pitcher for at least a full season, depending on the severity of the injury, due to corrective (Tommy John) surgery.

Modifications

Baseball fans entering the new century would soon experience an expanded postseason format, November baseball, and changes with the overall economic impact of the game. Implemented changes also sped up the pace of the game. Umpire calls in the field will now be challenged by team managers whereby the umpires leave their positions to confer via headphones with Major League Baseball Central in the Chelsea neighborhood of New York City. As noted already, both the number of home runs and the number of strikeouts increased each season, and defensive shifting has become more commonplace as well.

Baseball theorists have reason to believe that a new pitch will shift the balance of power back to the pitcher. Through the years, several new pitches developed: the knuckleball and the slider in the 1950s and 1960s and the split-fingered fastball in the 1970s to 1990s. Most recently, two pitches, the 100mph fastball coupled with a well-placed change-up, are the current trend to baffle the batter. As usual, it is the almighty home run that is of prime importance.

Diversity

In a recent statement from The World Economic Forum, Vijay Eswaran claimed that "diversity in the workplace is an asset for both businesses and their employees in its capacity to foster innovation, creativity, and empathy in ways that homogeneous environments seldom do." (4) However, political identity and nationalism may diametrically oppose this ideal. Eswaran added, "In this era of globalization, diversity in the business environment is about more than gender, race, and ethnicity." (5) Major League Baseball has been in the forefront of diversity and inclusion through various programs addressing those issues such as their "Diversity Pipeline program which seeks to identify, develop and grow the pool of qualified minority and female candidates for on-field and baseball operations positions throughout the industry." (6) Also, there have been substantial advancements for women in baseball administration. As reported by Alyson Footer in the May/June 2020 *Baseball Digest*, "For the past two years, MLB has sponsored a program called "Take the Field" that helps women prepare for opportunities that could eventually land them spots in roles typically saved for men: coaching, scouting and player development." (7) This program should not be confused with the National Baseball Hall of Fame's exhibit, "Taking the Field" that covers baseball's formative beginnings in an engaging interpretation that brings baseball's early years to life. (Mitch Wojnarowicz/National Baseball Hall of Fame and Museum) Other organizations that support and create opportunities for professional growth for young women starting in sports business such as WISE, (Women in Sports and Events), also make a concerted effort to have an impact at the grassroots level beyond sports.

MLB Globalization

The breadth of baseball has grown considerably on an international basis. On March 29, 2019, Major League Baseball announced via MLB News that "251 players represented 20 different countries and territories outside of the 50 United States on 2019 Opening Day 25-man rosters and inactive lists." (8) MLB International added, "For the 2019 season, MLB will work with 129 international media partners to broadcast games in 15 languages across 204 countries and territories. African Americans constitute 7.7% of the major leaguers' as white constitutes 57.5% as of 2017." (9)

The most critical factor in the growth of baseball today is globalization. Major League Baseball has already expanded to Japan and joined the National Basketball Association and the National Football League in Europe. Arguably, the greatest rivalry in professional sports is between the Boston Red Sox and the New York Yankees. The two teams recently brought America's national pastime to London, England, on June 29, 2019. Unlike the reception that Spalding received in his World Tour in England in 1888, as mentioned earlier, this tour appealed to much higher acclaim. Commissioner Manfred stated, "We hope this series will be the beginning of a relationship with London that persists and a continuation of increasing exposure for Major League Baseball in Europe." (10)

Major League Baseball Senior Vice President Jim Small was quoted in *USA Today* June 30, 2019, as saying, "All of the feedback was that [London] was fantastic. So, from a US standpoint, the pitching was not particularly good, the game was too long, but it was such a great fresh start for baseball here." (11) The *USA Today* Banner of June 30, 2019 read, the games were ridiculous, but MLB's London Series was a huge success. - Bob Nightengale (12)

The English tabloid offered their portrayal of the game in *The Guardian Today*, "Baseball is a cerebral and tightly focused game–much of apparently nothing punctuated by bursts of acceleration and deceleration–lost in London Stadium."(13)

Arguably, the recent London baseball series was a spectacle as opposed to a strategic match that European futbal (soccer) is all about. Ultimately, it remains to be seen whether there was a significant impact on the globalization of baseball in a most dynamic setting, London.

One may well ask why Major League Baseball is not playing the game in countries that are more tuned in to baseball, such as Italy, Germany, the Netherlands, South Korea, and Japan.

Although we have seen how baseball has been adversely affected in the United States, leading to a dip in its popularity, the game is proliferating beyond the reaches of American popular culture. For many reasons, other sports are on the rise in overall popularity in America. Football and basketball players can sign multi-million dollar contracts right after being drafted out of college. In contrast, baseball players typically do not see a pot of gold until they labor through the Minor League system and become free agents after six years in the big leagues.

Baseball requires several players to form a game, and there is also the need for baseball fields, leagues, and proper equipment that often are not available in inner cities. Also, it became cheaper to sign Latin-American talent and groom those players at the various academies Major League Baseball teams built across Latin America.

Nevertheless, "Baseball is more lucrative than it has ever been because of the continued escalation in the value of the sport's media rights and higher profits," Mike Ozanian of *Forbes* stated. (14) Due to the escalation of sport's media rights, Major League Baseball Advanced Media (MLBAM), baseball has enjoyed a continuous rise in profits. The Fox Network recently signed a new television contract from 2022 through the 2029 season, which has also encouraged the near future deals with Turner Broadcasting System (TBS) and the Entertainment and Sports Network (ESPN).

Thus, the continued rise in the value of media rights and higher profits has made significant contributions to the prosperity of Major League Baseball. Also, as stated in *Forbes*, "All Major League Baseball teams generated a record average operating income of $40 million during the 2018 season, 38% more than the previous year. Last season, revenue rose 4.8%, averaging $330 million per team, while player costs remained flat at $157 million." (15) Over the late 20thcentury, the increases in the average baseball team value have increased at an 11% annual rate of growth. At the same time, the National Basketball Association and National Football League team values have increased by 13 percent and 12 percent, respectively. (16)

Health Issues

In 1994, the government heard a scathing report by Senator Henry Waxman on the damages of tobacco use. At the Hearing on the Regulation of Tobacco Products House Committee on Energy and Commerce Subcommittee on Health and the Environment meeting on April 14, Representative Henry A. Waxman, chairman, made this opening statement:

> **This is an historic hearing. For the first time ever, the chief executive officers of our Nation's tobacco companies are testifying together before the US Congress. They are here because this subcommittee has legislative jurisdiction over those issues that affect our health. And no health issue is as important as cigarette smoking. It is sometimes easier to invent fiction than to face the truth. The truth is that cigarettes are the single most dangerous consumer product ever sold. Nearly a half-million Americans die every year as a result of tobacco. (17)**

Since then, baseball has tolerated the use of smokeless tobacco even though all medical data has proven its ill-effects. Unfortunately, today, we can still see some of the Major Leaguers with that omnipresent chaw in their cheek. In addition to these changes, Major League Baseball's crackdown on smokeless tobacco is taking effect only to a degree. From a report in *Sports Illustrated* July 2018, half of baseball's Major League teams have now banned smokeless tobacco. Until recently, chewing tobacco had achieved near ritual status even though tobacco had already been banned. Furthermore, "a growing number of cities take their action to ban smokeless tobacco from the ballpark as fewer current players are grandfathered under the league's policy," stated Emma Baccelieri in *Sports Illustrated* on July 23, 2018. (18)

The resilience of baseball is, once again, put to the test. At the beginning of 2020, a new insidious strain of a virus originated in China, traveled west, across Asia and into Europe before landing on our eastern doorstep. The world has not been the same since then. As of this writing, over 516,000 people succumbed to the ravages of the "Coronavirus" here in the United States. Currently, people are receiving vaccinations. Treatment medications are undergoing development and testing to thwart the advance of this devastating virus. All major sports were affected as their schedules adjusted to the demands of the virus. After arduous negotiations, the plan agreed on by the players and owners came to a 60-game season with restrictions beginning on July 23, 2020. James Wagner, *The New York Times*, wrote on June 29, 2020:

> **Coronavirus testing every other day for players and coaches. Wet rags for pitchers' pockets to prevent them from licking their fingers. Masks in the dugout and bullpen for any non-players. And no public transportation to the stadium, communal food spreads, saunas, fighting, spitting, smokeless tobacco, or sunflower seeds. (19)**

Wagner added:

> **To facilitate testing, the Sports Medicine Research and Testing Laboratory, which normally helps run the league's antidoping testing, has converted a portion of its facility in Salt Lake City for virus tests, promising a 24-hour turnaround on results. (20)**

And so it goes.

Museums

Following is a statement from the Executive Director of the Yogi Berra Museum & Learning Center on June 12, 2019:

Contemporary museums occupy an exciting place in our current cultural landscape as they have increasingly expanded their traditional role as repositories for static artifacts and assumed a more active role concerning the communities they engage in. In the case of the Yogi Berra Museum & Learning Center in Little Falls, NJ, we are committed to leveraging Yogi's great legacy as a vehicle for connecting visitors around the values he stood for: respect, teamwork, perseverance, and excellence. That commitment applies to all that the museum does whether it is engaging middle and high school students in conversations about racial equality through the lens of Major League Baseball's integration, providing military veterans and their supporters with pro bono assistance in honor of Yogi's World War II service at D-Day, or introducing immersive exhibitions like the state-of-the-art pitching installation PITCH that allows visitors of all ages and abilities to laugh and play together. (21)

The Mets Hall of Fame & Museum is an excellent attraction for all generations of Mets fans. It houses artifacts from special Mets moments, the 1969 and the 1986 World Series trophies, interactive kiosks, plaques for each member of the Mets Hall of Fame, and highlight videos celebrating the Mets most significant feats.

In a statement from Brian Richards, Curator of the New York Yankees Museum, on June 19, 2020, offered, the history of baseball—from the game's origins to the present day—cannot be understood without acknowledging the sport's "home" city. Beginning with the "New York Game" evolved on the streets of Manhattan and Brooklyn, baseball has risen into a global sport with New York City as its epicenter. No franchise better represents the City's fame and success than the New York Yankees. The heroes, teams, and achievements attained by the "Bronx Bombers" are celebrated inside the New York Yankees Museum. The Museum features both permanent and rotating exhibits honoring the Yankees' unparalleled success. Located inside Yankee Stadium, the Museum is open during home games and is a highlight of Yankee Stadium Tours. The Yankees' heritage of success lies at the heart of New York City's identity—and, by extension, at the heart of America's National Pastime. (22)

State of the Game

The Game Today - An Overview of a Challenging Time
State of the Game, Copywright Marty Appel 2019
Marty Appel, PR Director, New York Yankees, 1967-1976

Baseball has gone through—and survived—periods of apparent diminishing interest. In the late '60s and early '70s, everything about the game was flat, and one could argue that Tom Seaver, Johnny Bench, and Reggie Jackson were the only new players on the scene generating interest. Young people had moved on to other things, including the NFL and NBA. Muhammad Ali was the most intriguing athletic figure on the world stage.

Some thought baseball would be like opera—always there for the aging devotees but with a fan base not growing and in love with everything about the game's past.

However, the advent of modern marketing techniques, better television deals, and even small things like the production of *This Week in Baseball*, helped right the ship. The game went on to unimagined attendance highs, an influx of remarkable Latin American players, more fan-friendly ballparks, and the continuity of every game available on television.

Now to visit a ballpark is to see an enormous percentage of female attendance and of young fans—demographics who were not considered in play some 40 years ago. While TV ratings seem small (hundreds of stations offering competitive programming), the money paid for rights by networks and local providers is ever-growing, reflecting a belief that advertisers want to reach a baseball audience.

To many, the games feel too long, the strikeouts are too frequent, the wait diminishes the strategy for the long ball, and few stars have broken through to become national figures. Baseball has some genuine issues with which to deal. It is hard to call it the National Pastime anymore, but its growth internationally has been impressive, and one feels we are in another era that will transition into better times. It is just a part of the ebb and flow of a complex industry that sometimes needs to do some course corrections to retain its popularity.

Baseball from Bull Run to Baghdad
The National Pastime at War

By Jonathan Popovich

Throughout the history of the United States, few things are more closely associated with one another than our Military and our National Pastime. For nearly 160 years, generations of young Americans serving on the Homefront and abroad have relied upon the constancy of "our game" for morale, recreation, and physical fitness, and for its ability to heal and unify. In return, baseball has filled these roles more fully and completely than has any other national institution and has been doing so since the darkest days of the American experience.

The antebellum game of baseball, particularly the New York game, was becoming wildly popular in the Northeast and was even beginning its spread into the South prior to the start of our Civil War. Contrary to popular belief, it is likely that the onset of war may actually have hastened its more rapid spread, but nonetheless, it grew. Billy Yank and Johnny Reb found opportunities throughout that great national tragedy to pick nines and engage in countless matches of ball. In doing so, the military did what it has always done and pollinated pockets of people and culture with something new. In this case, Our National Pastime. One fine example of this was the game played at Hilton Head, South Carolina, on Christmas Day in 1862. A team from the 165th New York Volunteer

Infantry played against a picked nine in front of 40,000 onlookers. Such an event would have left a significant impression on even the most casual of "ballists" and helped seed the game's growth.

Soldiers returning to cities and farms of post-Civil War America did so with an increased familiarity and passion for baseball. For many who remained in uniformed service, they took these interests westward as our military began new campaigns on the Great Plains and in the deserts of the southwest. As a source of morale and physical fitness, military units began to ensure that their troopers were playing baseball. In saddle bags and pack trains throughout the West, these men stowed their bats and balls awaiting the chance to pick sides. Of the many military units and figures prominent in the 1870s, we need to look no further than Gen. George Custer's 7th Cavalry Regiment for an example of baseball's role within the ranks. The 7th Cav. fielded two clubs that played dozens of games between 1873 and 1876. Unfortunately for the men of the Actives and the Benteens, the ill-fated Battle of the Little Big Horn was their "final inning" afield.

As American history continued to unfold in the late 19th century, so too did the rich legacy of both baseball and the military. From western outposts in Arizona and the Dakotas to international ports in Africa and Latin America, the American servicemen turned to baseball as an escape from both the monotony of military drill and the stark reality of war. We know from newspaper accounts, diary entries, and a vast photographic record that baseball had become an integral part of soldiers' lives. One such example is the ball team fielded by the sailors of the USS *Maine*. Led by the pitching of their African American hurler, this group prevailed in the championship of the US Navy in 1897. They undoubtedly took their love of the game with them to Cuba where, just one year later, all but one team member would lose their life in service to the nation.

As our country's involvement in global matters grew in the 20th century, so too did the military's role in the protection and enforcement of our interests. In 1917 when the United States could no longer maintain its "Great War" neutrality, an American Expeditionary Force was sent abroad in support of our allies. The "Doughboys" that filled its ranks were passionate about the game of baseball. Training camps were established throughout France, and an entire department was set up by the military for the purpose of morale, welfare, and recreation. To support this, hundreds of thousands of pieces of baseball equipment in the form of bats, balls, gloves, and catchers' gear were shipped overseas by organizations such as the YMCA and Knights of Columbus. During downtime, baseball was being played by American Servicemen throughout France, and many units fielded organized teams that played for major championships.

It was also during this time that baseball and military symbolism became forever linked. Images of Uncle Sam began popping up on scorecards and sporting goods catalogs. Professional clubs began wearing American flag patches and patriotic armbands on their uniforms. They even began to conduct on-field military drills with their bats in support of the boys overseas.

For the first time, the nexus of baseball and the military did not just involve amateur players and enthusiasts. Seventy-six Major Leaguers, including some of the game's biggest stars, like Grover Cleveland Alexander, Harry Gowdy, Ty Cobb, and Christy Mathewson, also answered the call to service. Tragically, one former player, the NY Giants' Eddie Grant, was killed in action during combat operations in France.

As important as baseball was to those in the foxhole, it may have been just as meaningful to morale on the Homefront. By the time the final shots of WWI were fired on Nov. 11, 1918, over 116,000 American soldiers had lost their lives. Baseball had provided a refuge of sorts to an aching public who had sent their young people off to war. One enduring example of how military pride and patriotism intersected with baseball happened during the 1918 World Series. During Game 1, and for the first time at a baseball game, the Star-Spangled Banner was performed in acknowledgment of our servicemen's sacrifices abroad.

Baseball in the wake of WWI saw a revolution taking place within the sport. While the Black Sox scandal of 1919 threatened to cripple the institution, the meteoric rise of Babe Ruth saved and changed the game forever. At the same time, a downsized military returned to the rhythm of stateside drill and ceremony which, of course, allowed "Joe" to participate in his pastime of choice.

There is a voluminous record of amateur baseball games being played within the military during the 1920s and 1930s. Countless teams from just as many different units played at every fort and installation across the nation and overseas. While the military paced itself for two decades of relative peace, professional baseball spent the same time gaining in popularity, yet struggling for profits due to the Great Depression. Despite the shared challenges being endured by the entire country, some of the game's greatest teams and players rose to prominence in the period between the World Wars. However, the world itself was hurtling toward unparalleled disaster.

Germany's 1939 invasion of Poland initiated the greatest armed conflict in human history. In 1940, the United States began to prepare for the inevitable by implementing its first ever peace time draft, while baseball was about to enjoy one of its finest campaigns to date. In 1941, Joe DiMaggio hit in 56 consecutive games while his rival in Boston, Ted Williams, hit over .400—the last man to reach that plateau. On October 6th of the storied season, the Yankees defeated the Dodgers in the World Series. Just two months later Pearl Harbor was attacked, and the United States was at war once again.

Young men from every walk of life began to enlist by the hundreds of thousands. One of baseball's biggest stars—the 1940 American League MVP Hank Greenberg—was the first professional to swap out uniforms when he joined the Army. Hundreds of Major Leaguers followed suit including DiMaggio, Williams, and Musial. Thousands of Minor Leaguers would also answer the call to arms. With a world in chaos, how significant could baseball possibly be to the war effort? As it turned out, vitally important.

In early 1942, the Commissioner of Baseball reached out to President Roosevelt for guidance on how the game should operate, if at all, during such crisis. FDR thought that baseball could and should proceed, as its morale boost for the millions of servicemen and civilians involved in the war effort was important. The president's wisdom opened the door for baseball's most significant contributions to the military and the nation during its 150-year existence.

With nearly all the past season's rosters now serving in the military, baseball—as a sport, not an organization—was forced to get creative. Older or former professionals filled in for those at war. The All-American Girls Professional Baseball League was formed, and many of the defense plants and military units again raised teams of their own. Night games gained in popularity as it allowed for those working in factories to relax after long shifts producing the tools of war.

On the Homefront, baseball was providing a much-needed respite for the civilian population backing the war effort. Within the ranks, most of the game's stars continued to play while in service. Many played on teams comprised of Major and Minor Leaguers during a host of exhibition contests held for the enjoyment of the troops. A handful of professionals such as Warren Spahn, Bob Feller, Ralph Houk, Jerry Coleman, Yogi Berra, and Monte Irvin actually saw combat. Two Major Leaguers, Elmer Gedeon and Harry O'Neill, made the ultimate sacrifice, as did hundreds of Minor Leaguers and collegiate players.

Clearly, the members of baseball's professional ranks were contributing to the fight. However, there were millions of other servicemen who went off to war with a love of baseball as strong as those who would eventually make the Hall of Fame. What of their contributions and the role that baseball played in their life and death struggles?

There was not a soldier, sailor, airman, or marine who did not engage in a game of baseball at some point during their service between 1941 and 1945. Baseball was played on English country sides and in French villages, in African deserts and on airstrips of Pacific Islands. It was even played on the decks of battleships and aircraft carriers at sea. Who has not seen the images of GIs with a glove or bat stuffed in their packs as they boarded troop ships or trucks to the front? Who has not seen a movie about the war where soldiers were gathered around a radio listening to a game?

President Roosevelt's encouragement of Major League Baseball during WWII was a way for those on the Homefront to briefly escape the daily reminders of war. The establishment of military baseball leagues provided an opportunity for the biggest stars to keep playing while still serving their country. The passion for the game allowed for women to break into organized, professional baseball during this time, and for the long overdue integration of military teamsyears before baseball's color barrier was broken stateside.

Baseball was a salve for those who experienced the physical and emotional wounds of combat and an escape for the millions that welcomed them home. The Game had served honorably during the war and, unfortunately, would have to do so again soon.

In the wake of WWII, baseball experienced a resurgence and enjoyed what many call the game's "Golden Era." The mighty Yankees established a dynasty that had not been seen before or since. Stars like Mickey Mantle, Willie Mays, and Duke Snider became the idols of boys everywhere. And the 1947 undoing of the oppressive "Gentlemen's Agreement" by Branch Rickey and Jackie Robinson finally allowed baseball to truly become Our National Pastime.

Between the Great Depression and WWII, the United States experienced over 15 years of challenges and triumphs. There seemed to be a general sense of ease and good feeling during the 1950s, but this feeling belied the next conflict that would ultimately result in the deaths of over 54,000 American servicemen.

The Korean War has been termed the "Forgotten War," but for those who served there—particularly those who saw combat—nothing is further from the truth. That conflict was waged on the most demanding of terrains, in the harshest of climates, and in the face of a fierce and determined enemy. Despite these circumstances, Korea was going to be a limited action as far as the politics involved were concerned. The widespread conscriptions and enlistments seen during WWII did not happen this time and baseball, like many other institutions, was left largely intact as a result. Between 1950 and 1953, most clubs lost few, if any at all, players to the service.

That said, the mighty Yankees were without the services of Whitey Ford, Bobby Brown, and Billy Martin for parts of three seasons, while their cross-town rivals, the Dodgers and Giants, missed the presence of Don Newcombe and Willie Mays respectively.

Of the players who did enter into service during Korea, most never saw the front lines. Two notable exceptions to this were Marine Corps Flyers Ted Williams and Gerry Coleman. Both were called out of reserves and back to active duty during the war and were decorated for their participation in numerous combat missions in the skies over Korea. One former big leaguer and WWII Veteran, Bob Neighbors of the St. Louis Browns, was killed in action.

While the conduct of the Korean War was largely dissimilar to WWII in terms of military and political strategy, the experience of the soldiers on the ground might well have been the same. Called upon by their country to do a job, they were young men far from their homes in the most unforgiving of environments. The combat they experienced was up close, all too personal, and left little time for rest and recovery. When they did have down time, there again was baseball.

Pickup games popped up at camps a mere few hundred yards from the constantly moving front lines, and Armed Forces Radio regularly aired broadcasts of stateside baseball games for the enjoyment and morale of the troops. However, there was a change afoot as far as baseball's role in the military was concerned. A change defined by a shift from the individual player's participation to ardent support that continues to this day.

Following Korea, it was not a full decade before the United States was again embroiled in armed conflict. Our 10-year odyssey in Vietnam brought with it new challenges never experienced by those we sent off to war. The lack of popular support on the Homefront left the fighting man devoid of the simple vestiges of morale enjoyed by his fathers and grandfathers. It was a guerilla war fought without front lines, and the pace of operations aided by advancements in mobility didn't allow most troops the luxury of time or space in which to do much of anything, let alone organize a pickup game of baseball. Quite simply, most locales in Vietnam were not safe enough for recreation given the tactics and strategy of the enemy.

Changes to the draft process and alternate avenues of service afforded virtually all Major League players a way around active duty in Vietnam. There were, however, several big leaguers who did serve in Vietnam including Jim Bibby, Al Bumbry, Ed Figueroa, Bobby Jones, and Gary Maddux. Two players, Chuck Goggin, and Roy Gleason, both of the L.A. Dodgers, were wounded in action there.

While the rosters of Major League clubs were no longer supplying manpower to the military, the organization remained as supportive as ever. In 1967, the USO in collaboration with MLB organized a trip of current and former stars to Vietnam. That year Pete Rose, Joe DiMaggio, Jerry Coleman, and Tony Conigliaro toured the warzone and visited with troops throughout the south of the country. In 1968 Hall of Famer Ernie Banks followed suit.

Like generations before them, it is reasonable to assume that many of those young people serving in Vietnam did so with an interest in baseball. Combat tours were set at 12-13 months, so a baseball enthusiast might only miss one season of their favorite team's exploits. Given all the chaos and upheaval going on in America during Vietnam, it's possible that baseball might have been the only reliable constant for many of the returning veterans and something that he or she could have used to help manage the deep emotional scars of war.

Since the end of American involvement in Vietnam in 1973, the United States has continued to see its share of conflict. In the past 50 years, American servicemen and woman have been called to action all over the world. Latin America, the Middle East, and Africa are just a few of the places they have fought and died in the name of freedom. Wherever they have gone, baseball in one form or another has been a companion, an escape, and a morale booster. I can say this, because when I deployed to Iraq in 2003, not a day went by that I did not think or talk baseball with one of my buddies. Of the many critical things that I needed to have with me over there, I made room in my pack for a baseball glove. I had a ball mailed to me that all the guys in my unit signed. It will forever remain a valued memory and keepsake. As will the clipped box scores and sports pages that my parents and grandmother sent along in their care packages. So yes, baseball meant a great deal to me over there, and it continues to mean a lot to those men and women serving today, as well as those waiting for them back home.

In 2016, MLB and the US Army collaborated on the first ever professional baseball game played on an active military installation. That contest, a rousing success and showcase of two of America's greatest institutions, was held at Fort Bragg, NC. Each season, and at every ballpark across the country, baseball recognizes and honors our nation's military and veterans. From military appreciation day to "veteran of the game" events, Our National Pastime in many forms remains at the forefront of support for our nation's truest heroes.

About the essayist:

Jonathan Popovich is a combat veteran of the war in Iraq, and currently serves as the Director for the Vet Center in New Jersey. He has written two books on vintage baseball equipment, is a donor and contributor to the National Baseball Hall of Fame, and a docent at the Yogi Berra Museum and Learning Center. He is an active member of the Society for American Baseball Research and has presented at the past four 19th Century Research Conferences in Cooperstown, NY. He has been named the "Veteran of the Game" by both the NY Yankees and NY Mets and was the NY Yankees' military representative to MLB and PEOPLE magazine's "Tribute for Heroes" event at the 2013 MLB All-Star Game.

Epilogue

As I researched the thought evolving around the origins of baseball, it became clear to me that New York City would be at its epicenter throughout these past two centuries. With the United States experiencing unprecedented growth entering the 19th century by way of the market revolution, the shift from an agrarian society into urbanization opened the door to life in the city. Industrialization through mechanization was a prime factor for urban development. Baseball moved in lock step with the cities' growth, having a profound effect on our country's popular culture. From early folk games to town ball to organized games of 'ball' arising mostly in the northeastern sector of the country, it was the 'Knickerbocker' game, popularized in New York in 1845 that became the centerpiece of organized baseball. In addition, the city of Brooklyn also became a hotbed further enhancing the attraction in the metropolitan area, which became a great intercity rivalry. (Brooklyn was incorporated into the New York City charter when the city consolidated the five boroughs in 1898). The development of train travel and the telegraph in the 1830s and 1840s were main factors in spreading the game. By this time, New York City became the center of finance, art, theater, the press, and commerce, in addition to the burgeoning sport-baseball.

New York coalesced baseball and American history from its early beginnings of the organized game. Through Manifest Destiny, the Gold Rush, the Civil War and the unification thereafter, Segregation/Integration, Tammany Hall, the Gilded Age, Progressivism, the Roaring 20s, World War II, the Golden Era of New York Baseball, free agency, work stoppages (strikes and lockouts), scandals, baseball and US history have now moved into the 21st Century. What is clear is how the resilience of the national pastime overcame major setbacks while preparing to face its most serious test—the Coronavirus. What isn't clear is the road to recovery.

Dr. Gabriel Vitalone Interview

Dr. Vitalone, Professor Emeritus at William Paterson University, is a retired teacher and educator, having taught on all levels from preschool through university graduate school.

I had the pleasure of speaking with Dr. Gabriel Vitalone at his home in Pompton Lakes, New Jersey, on November 20, 2019. Gabe, as he prefers to be called, is very spry and lucid at 97 years of age. (Imagine running a marathon at 93 as did Gabe.) He recalled witnessing Babe Ruth play in 1927! His dad had then taken him to his first game at Yankee Stadium, and he was smitten.

Gabe spoke of the tough times growing up in Yonkers, NY, during the hardships of the Depression. He remembered the nickel it cost him for the trolley ride to the Bronx where he picked up the subway for another nickel that took him to the Stadium when he was old enough to venture to the ballpark unescorted in 1936. Joe DiMaggio had come to the Yankees in that year, helping them win the first World Series after a three-year drought and three more wins immediately thereafter. Gabe's favorite player at the time was Lou Gehrig because as great as he was, Gehrig always seemed to be playing second fiddle to Babe Ruth.

Gabe recalled the hardships of his Italian heritage in those years as the Italians were still looked down upon since their mass immigration in the 1890s. Too poor to attend games, Gabe often listened to the games on the radio. Gabe found a hero in Joe DiMaggio. "Being of the same heritage, he became our patron saint," Gabe said. Ethnicity was coming into full view at the time. The Jewish people were also looked askance until a Bronxite, Hank Greenberg, started playing professional baseball in that same era and was elected to the Baseball Hall of Fame.

Gabe attended Fordham University in 1941, joined the Marines, and entered the US Army ASTP-ROTC program. As an officer, he led his squad into heavy action during World War II in the Ardennes Forest during the Battle of the Bulge under General Patton, the same battle that former Yankees' catcher and manager, Ralph Houk had also valiantly fought in.

One of Gabe's favorite memories was purchasing the first bleacher ticket, (a boyhood dream that he coveted and fulfilled), while in his uniform, to the 1943 World Series.

Gabe is spending his time now writing his memoirs. He recently fulfilled a childhood dream of singing the national anthem at Yankee Stadium.

NOTES

PART ONE:

Chapter 1 - Post-Revolutionary War Era

1. https://www.history.com/topics/inventions/cotton-gin-and-eli-whitney

2. Ibid.

3. Eliot J. Gorn and Warren Goldstein, *A Brief History of American Sports; Second edition* University of Illinois Press 20130,43.

4. https://sabr.org/latest/1791-baseball-in-pittsfield-mass/

5. https://study.com/academy/lesson/the-market-revolution-in-america-definition-lesson-quiz.html

6. https://courses.lumenlearning.com/boundless-ushistory/chapter/the-market-revolution/

7. Steven A. Riess, *City Games: The Evolution of American Urban Society and the Rise of Sports* (Illini Books Edition of the University of Illinois, 1991),46.

8. Ibid.

9. George Thompson, *National Advocate*, April 25, 1823, page 2, column 4. "New York Baseball, 1823," The New York Times

10. Edited by Peter Morris, William J. Ryczek, Jan Finkel, Leonard Levin and Richard Malatzky *Base Ball Founders: The Clubs, Players and Cities of the Northeast That Established the Game* (McFarland

and Company, Inc., Publishers, 2013), New York Base Ball Club (a.k.a. Washington BBC, Gotham BBC) (John Thorn) 46.

11. George B. Kirsch, *Baseball in Blue and Gray (*Princeton University Press, 2001), xii-xiv.

12. William J. Ryczek, *Baseball's First Inning: A history of the National Pastime through the Civil War* (McFarland and Company, 2009*)*, 28.

13. John Thorn, *Baseball in the Garden of Eden: The Secret History of the Early Game* (Simon and Schuster, 2011), 38,39.

14. http://www.19cbaseball.com/game.html

15. George Kirsch, *The Creation of American Team Sports*First Edition (University of Illinois Press,1989), 10.

16. Charles Alexander, *Our Game-An American Baseball History* (Henry Holt and Company, New York, 1991),8.

Chapter 2 – Organized Base Ball

1. Elizabeth L. Bradley, *Knickerbocker-The Myth Behind New York* Rivergate Books 2009; p27

2. John Thorn, *Baseball in the Garden of Eden: The Secret History of the Early Game* (Simon & Schuster, 2011), 42.

3. Steven A. Riess, *City Games: The Evolution of American Urban Society and the Rise of Sports* (The University of Illinois Press, 1991), 1.

4. Benjamin Rader, *Baseball – A History of America's Game*, 3rd ed. (University of Illinois, 2008), 2.

5. Ed Rielly, *Baseball; An Encyclopedia of Popular Culture*, ABC-CLIO Inc., 110.

6. https://courses.lumenlearning.com/boundless-ushistory/chapter/manifest-destiny/

7. https://riversprojectweek.weebly.com/impacts.html

8. Kimberly   McGees://www.theclassroom.com/political-party-opposed-idea-manifest-destiny-11585.html

9. Jonathan Kirsch, Sept. 19, 2004, https://www.latimes.com/archives/la-xpm-2004-sep-19-bk-kirsch19-story.html

10. John Thorne, https://ourgame.mlblogs.com/the-knickerbockers-san-franciscos-first-base-ball-team-part-two-bb71094011e7

Chapter 3 – The National Pastime

1. John Thorn, *Our Game*; Spring 2011 issue;https://ourgame.mlblogs.com/the-new-york-game-in-1856-6c58bdd4a420

2. Dean Sullivan, *Early Innings-A Documentary History of Baseball, 1825-1908,* University of Nebraska Press 1995, p22

3. George Kirsch, *The Creation of American Team Sports;* University of Illinois Press; First Edition, 1989, p58

4. Andrew Schiff, SABR – *The National Pastime Volume 28,* 2008, p26

5. Ibid.

6. Paul Goldberger's, *Ballpark; Baseball in the American City;* Alfred A. Knopf, New York (2019) v11

7. John Thorn, *Baseball in the Garden of Eden, The Secret History of the Early Game.* Simon & Schuster; 2011, p117

8. Ed Rielly, *"BASEBALL: An Encyclopedia of Popular Culture"* ABC-CLIO, Santa Barbara, CA, p110

9. Tony Morante, *Baseball and Tammany Hall,* SABR – Spring 2013 ed. P30

10. John Adler with Draper Hill, *Doomed by Cartoon; How Cartoonist Thomas Nast and The New York Times Brought down Boss Tweed and His Ring of Thieves;* Morgan James, Garden City, NY, 2008, p3

11. Michael Beschloss, https://www.nytimes.com/2014/09/27/upshot/the-longest-game-williams-vs-amherst.html

12. https://www.ncaa.com/news/baseball/article/2019-07-01/story-first-ever-college-baseball-game-1859

13. https://en.wikipedia.org/wiki/College_baseball

14. Daniel R. Epstein, https://tht.fangraphs.com/the-stop-and-start-history-of-womens-baseball/https://en.wikipedia.org/wiki/College_baseball

15. Ibid.

16. Ellen Klages, https://www.exploratorium.edu/baseball/features/girls-of-the-summer.html.

Chapter 4 – The Civil War Era

1. George P. Kirsch, *Baseball in Blue and Gray; The National Pastime During the Civil War,* Princeton University Press, (2003) p18

2. Joel Zoss and John Bowman, *Diamonds in the Rough: The Untold History of Baseball*, MacMillan Publishing Company of New York, 1989 p234 "The National Game. Three 'Outs' And One 'Run,'" from *Harper's Weekly* on September 15, 1860.

3. Ibid.

4. Larry Bowman, Soldiers at Play: *Baseball on the American Frontier-for Nine: A Journal of Baseball History and Culture* p36,7

5. George P. Kirsch, *Baseball in Blue and Gray; The National Pastime During the Civil War,* Princeton University Press, (2003) p119

6. https://constitutioncenter.org/blog/on-this-day-lincolns-emancipation-proclamation-changes-history

7. http://totallyhistory.com/enrollment-act-of-1863/

8. http://ushistoryscene.com/article/baseball-and-the-civil-war/ by Zachary Brown,

9. https://www.loc.gov/pictures/item/94508290/

10. George B. Kirsch, *Baseball in Blue & Gray*, Princeton University, 2003, p 125

11. Ibid, p124, 127

12. https://catto.ushistory.org/catto-and-american-civil-rights/

13. https://en.wikipedia.org/wiki/Jim_Crow_laws

14. LOC, *Baseball Americana*, 2009, p35

15. Ibid.

16. John Thorn, *Baseball in the Garden ofEden*; p189,190

17. https://fordhamsports.com/roster.aspx?rp_id=1294

18. Mitch Wojnarowicz/National Baseball Hall of Fame and Museum

Chapter 5 – Professional Baseball and the Gilded Age

1. Bill Ferber, ed, *Inventing Baseball, The 100 Greatest Games of the Nineteenth Century*, SABR, 2013, p79

2. Charles Alexander, *Our Game: An American Baseball History* Henry Holt, 1991, p26

3. https://www.history.com/topics/19th-century/gilded-age

4. Esther Crain, *The Gilded Age in New York 1870-1910,* Black Dog and Leventhal Publishers, 2016, p7

5. Ibid.

6. Idem

7. Daniel Czitrom, *New York Exposed – The Gilded Age Police Scandal that Launched the Progressive Era."* Oxford University Press, 2016, p133,4

8. http://www.loc.gov/teachers/classroommaterials/presentationsandactivities/presentations/timeline/riseind/

9. Ibid.

10. https://www.baseball-reference.com/bullpen/Reserve_clause

11. Home / Sports Card News / Vintage Sports Card News / Peck and Snyder: As a sporting goods store, Peck & Snyder sold baseball equipment and supplies. Producing baseball cards as advertising material fit right in with the business they had already established. Other businesses, in an attempt to capitalize on the growing marketing trend, soon followed suit. They started distributing baseball cards with advertisements for their companies printed on the back even when their companies had absolutely nothing to do with baseball or athleticism. Cigarette cards like Old Judge and Allen & Ginter gained popularity before the century was over. Today, the cards are incredibly scarce and considered truly historical relics. In order to promote baseball to a worldwide audience, Irving Snyder joined Chicago sporting goods owner and ex-baseball pitcher A.G. Spaulding on a world tour in 1888.

Chapter 6 – The National League

1. Leonard Koppett, *Major League Baseball,* Carroll & Graf Publishers, New York 2004 p25,26

2. https://www.baseball-reference.com/bullpen/Reserve_clause

3. John Thorn, *Baseball in the Garden of Eden*, p207

4. spaldingbros.com/it_en/storia/

5. Harold Seymour, *Baseball the Early Years,* Oxford University Press 1960 p8,9

6. David Nemec, *The Beer and Whiskey League* Lyon & Burford (1994) p16

7. Ibid., p70

8. Ed Rielly, (italicize book title) Baseball An Encyclopedia of Popular Culture; ABC-CLIO, Inc. 2000 p 155

9. Peter Morris, William Ryczek, Jay Finkel, Leonard Levn, AND Richard Maltzky *Base Ball FoundersMcFarland and Company, 2013 p251 Jared Wheeler*

10. Ibid., p253

11. https://courses.lumenlearning.com/boundless-ushistory/9/the-progressive-era/

12. https://www.britannica.com/biography/Jacob-Riis

13. Peter Panacy, *Bleacher Report*, "Major League Baseball Finds Its Roots in Progressive America." April 11, 2011

14. https://americasfavoritepasttime.weebly.com/original/baseball-during-the-progressive-era

15. Charles Alexander, *Our Game; An American Baseball History*, Henry Holt and Company, 1991, p38

16. Ibid., p55

17. Melvin Adelman, *A Sporting Time; New York City and the Rise of Modern Athletics* University of Illinois Press (1986) p2

PART TWO:

Chapter 7 – The American League

1. Oliver Allen, *New York, New York;* New York MacMillan Publishing, 1990 p180

2. Ibid.

3. Terry Golway, *Machine Made; Tammany Hall and the Creation of Modern American Politics*; W.W. Norton & Company Ltd. (2014) p167

4. Tony Morante, *The Baseball Research Journal*, SABR, Spring 2013, p34

5. Frank Graham, *The New York Giants: An Unofficial History of a Great Baseball Club*, The Southern Illinois University Press Series. P18

6. Ibid., p26

7. Idem

8. Steven A. Riess, *Touching Base-Professional Baseball and American Culture in the Progressive Era* University of Illinois Press, 1985, p74,75

9. Eddie Frierson, SABR https://sabr.org/bioproj/person/christy-mathewson/

10. Marty Appel, *Pinstripe Empire*, Bloomsbury Press, 2012, p17,18

11. https://m.facebook.com/PDNYHistoryInColor/posts/2076412322381117 Sgt. Michael Bosak, NYPD historian, reported that, "on January8th, 1877, when Ptl. John McDowell and two other police officers , Max Schmittberger and Alexander "Clubber" Williams passed out in a bar on Seventh Ave. in New York City from heavy drinking very early in the morning. McDowell heard a commotion and arose to find three burglars coming through the skylight when he was shot behind his left ear. He captured one, but, the two others got away. For this action, McDowell was awarded a silver medal of honor minted by Tiffany & Co. The NY logo that sat atop the medal became globally renown.

12. Donald Honig, *The American League, An Illustrated History*, Crown Publishers, Inc. New York 1983, p5

13. Robert Thompson, Tim Wiles, Andy Strasberg*Baseball's Greatest Hit: The Story of "Take Me Out to the Ball Game"* Hal Leonard Corporation; Har/Com edition (April 2, 2008)

Chapter 8 – The Jacob Ruppert Era

1. Glenn Stout, *Yankees Century*, Houghton Mifflin, 2002 p67

2. Ibid.

3. Idem

4. Ed Rielly, "*BASEBALL: An Encyclopedia of Popular Culture*" p283 Years, 1903-1915

5. Bill Francis, https://baseballhall.org/discover/1918-flu-pandemic-didnt-spare-baseball

6. Glenn Stout, *Yankees Century.* p83

7. Ibid.

8. Interview with Max Frazee

9. David Pietrusza, *Rothstein, The Life and Times of the Criminal Genius Who Fixed the 1919 World Series* Carroll & Graf Publishers, New York (2003) p149

10. Ed Rielly, *"BASEBALL: An Encyclopedia of Popular Culture"* p32

Chapter 9 – The Roaring Twenties

1. Lloyd Johnson, *Baseball's Book of Firsts*; Brompton Books (1999) p162

2. Ibid.

3. Ed Rielly, *"BASEBALL: An Encyclopedia of Popular Culture"*; p251

4. Ibid.

5. Idem p218

6. John Holway, *Josh, and Satch: The Life and Times of Josh Gibson and Satchel Paige,* Carroll & Graf Publishers, New York, 1991 p22

7. John Thorn, *SABR 2011 Baseball Research Journal*, Henry Chadwick Award: John B. Holway p124.

John B. Holway has been a baseball researcher since 1944. After a stint as a parachute lieutenant in Korea, he wrote the first book in English on Japanese baseball, *Japan Is Big League in Thrills*, in 1954. The next year he penned Sumo, the first English book on that subject.

Since then he has served as an economics analyst for the Voice of America, covered conferences around the world, written for major newspapers from Boston to San Diego, and covered the Olympic Games in Mexico

City and Los Angeles and World Series from 1948 through 1986. He published a major oral history of the Tuskegee Airmen, *Red Tails, Black Wings: The Men of America's Black Air Force* (1997).

John B. Holway has published many notable books on the Negro Leagues, perhaps most notably *Voices from the Great Black Baseball Leagues* (1975), It is not too much to say that without John Holway's efforts, several Negro League stars would not have entered the Baseball Hall of Fame when they did. John Thorn

Chapter 10 – The Depression Era

1. Thorn, Palmer, Gershman & Pietrusza, *Total Baseball, 6th ed.*, Total Sports, New York 1999 p107

2. Bill Bryson, *The Babe Didn't Point,* Iowa State University Press, 1986 p7

3. Ed Rielly, *"BASEBALL: An Encyclopedia of Popular Culture"*; p11

4. www.bguthriephotos.com › keys › 2018_DC_LOC_Baseball

5. Stout, *Yankees Century* pp172,173

6. Jonathan Fraser Light, *The Cultural Encyclopedia of Baseball;* MacFarland and Company, 1997. p 234

7. Ibid., p311

8. Bert Sugar, *Bert Sugar's Baseball Hall of Fame; A History of America's Greatest Game* Running Press Book Publishers (2009), p15

9. Daniel Slotnik, https://www.nytimes.com/2017/11/09/obituaries/ray-robinson-who-wrote-of-gehrig-the-man-dies-at-96.html

10. Marty Appel, *Pinstripe Empire*, Bloomsbury (2014), p210

Chapter 11 – The War Years

1. Robert Creamer, *Baseball-and Other Matters in 1941*; First Bison Books, 1991 p3

2. Edward J. Rielly, ed., *Baseball and American Culture,* The Hayworth Press, 2003, p132

3. Benjamin Rader, *Baseball-A History of America's Game*; Illini Books, 1994 p.xvi

4. Peter Golenbock (2002). *Bums: An Oral History of the Brooklyn Dodgers.* Mineola, New York: Dover Publications. pp. 44–46. IS

5. Zoss, Joel, and John Bowman, *Diamonds in the Rough: The Untold History of Baseball*, MacMillan Publishing Company of New York, 1989 p98

6. Ibid.

7. https://www.aagpbl.org/history/league-history

8. https://baseballhall.org/discover-more/stories/baseball-history/league-of-women-ballplayers

9. Benjamin Rader, p156,

10. Robert F. Burk, *Much More Than a Game,* The University of North Carolina Press, 2001, *p73*

11. Michael Haupert, https://eh.net/encyclopedia/the-economic-history-of-major-league-baseball/

Chapter 12 – New York's Glory Days

1. Edward Robb Ellis, *The Epic of New York City – A Narrative History* – Old Town Books, 1990. P453

2. *The New York Times, April 16, 1947, in Sports of the Times*: Play Ball!

   In addition, Dodgers' manager, Leo Durocher was suspended for marrying actress Laraine Day, before she was divorced causing an uproar, especially in the Catholic church.

3. Ibid.

4. Louis Efrat, The *New York Times*, April 27th, 1947

5. Roberta Newman and Joel Rosen, *Black Baseball, Black Business-Race Enterprise and the Fate of the Segregated Dollar*; The University Press of Mississippi, 2014, p155

6. Ibid.

7. Glenn Stout, *Yankees Century* Houghton Mifflin Company, p210

8. Burt Solomon, *The Baseball Timeline in Association with Major League Baseball*; DK Publishing, Inc. 2001, p480

9. Noel Hynd, *The Giants of the Polo Grounds*, Doubleday New York, 1988 p367

10. Ibid., p368

11. Sal Yvars, Giants catcher at a Westchester, NY SABR meeting

12. Richard McElvey, *The MacPhails: baseball's first family of the front office*, MacFarland and Co. 2000 p116

13. Ibid.

14. Louis Effrat, *The New York Times* March 19, 1953

15. Joseph M. Sheehan, *The New York Times*, September 30, 1953

16. https://www.scpr.org/news/2008/06/24/2554/walter-omalley-was-influential-bringing-dodgers-la/

17. A. Bartlett Giamatti, *Take Time for Paradise: Americans and Their Games* Summit Books, Simon & Schuster, 1989, p49

18. Peter Golenbock, *Bums: An Oral History of the Brooklyn Dodgers*; G.P. Putnam & Sons, 1984 p441

19. Ibid., p442

Chapter 13 – Expansion

1. Jonathan Fraser Light, *The Cultural Encyclopedia of Baseball*, McFarland & Company, Inc., 1997 p237

2. Dean Sullivan, ed. *"Late Innings: A Documentary History of Baseball, 1945-1972,* University of Nebraska p156

3. Charles Alexander, *Our Game*, Henry Holt and Company, 1991, p246,247

4. https://timesmachine.nytimes.com/timesmachine/1964/08/14/issue.html

5. Ibid.

6. Alexander, Our Game, p255

7. https://baseballhall.org/discover-more/stories/short-stops/pfister-papers-give-inside-look-at-mlb-draft

8. www.mlbplayers.com

9. Ibid.

10. http://www.seanlahman.com/baseball-archive/brief-history-of-baseball

11. www.mlbplayers.com

12. Ibid.

13. https://www.theatlantic.com/entertainment/archive/2011/07/how-curt-flood-changed-baseball-and-killed-his-career-in-the-process/241783/ by Allen Barra

14. https://www.mlb.com/news/negro-leagues-celebrating-100th-anniversary Bill Ladson, Feb.14, 2020

Chapter 14 – The Turbulent Seventies

1. Jonathan Fraser Light, *The Cultural Encyclopedia of Baseball*, McFarland & Company, Inc., 1997 p699

2. Ibid.

3. Marty Appel, *Pinstripe Empire*, Bloomsbury, 2014

4. Glenn Stout, *Yankees Century* Houghton Mifflin, Company, 2002, p316

5. Sam Roberts, *New York Times* Dec. 6, 2015 fromhttps://sabr.org/research/turbulent-70s-steinbrenner-stadium-and-1970s-scene

6. Marty Appel, *Pinstripe Empire*, Bloomsbury, 201Pp 389, 390

7. https://sabr.org/research/turbulent-70s-steinbrenner-stadium-and-1970s-scene

8. Ibid.

9. https://bleacherreport.com/articles/154265-come-to-think-of-it-the-day-that-changed-major-league-baseball-forever

10. Appel, *Pinstripe Empire*, p432

11. Marty Appel, *Munson: The Life and Death of a Yankee Captain*, Anchor, 2010., p257.

12. Telephone interview with Ms. Joan Gianmarino

Chapter 15 – The 1980s – A Decade of Transition

1. Jonathan Fraser Light, *The Cultural Encyclopedia of Baseball*; McFarland & Co. 1997, p700

2. Marvin Miller, *A Whole Different Ball Game; The Sport and Business of Baseball* Carol Publishing Group (1991) p318

3. Dan D'Addona, *SABR Fall 2011 Baseball Research Journal*

4. Marvin Miller, *A Whole Different Ball Game; The Sport and Business of Baseball* Carol Publishing Group (1991) p391,392

5. Babicz and Zeiler, *National Pastime; U.S. History Through Baseball* Rowan and Littlefield, 2017, p168

6. https://www.history.com/topics/natural-disasters-and-environment/1989-san-francisco-earthquake

7. https://www.nytimes.com/1989/09/02/obituaries/giamatti-scholar-and-baseball-chief-dies-at-51.html Robert McFadden, September 2, 1989

8. https://mason.gmu.edu/~rmatz/giamatti.html

Chapter 16 – The 1990s

1. Jonathan Fraser Light, *The Cultural Encyclopedia of Baseball*; McFarland & Co. 1997, p700

2. Martin C. Babicz and Thomas W. Zeiler, *National Pastime: U.S. History Through Baseball*, Rowman & Littlefield, 2017, p171

3. Elliot J. Gorn and Warren Goldstein, *A Brief History of American Sports,* University of Illinois Press, 2013, p260

4. Mark Fainaru-Wada and Lance Williams, *Game of Shadows* Penguin Group – New York City 2006 p72

5. https://www.faithandfreedom.com/baseball-america-and-the-21st-century

6. ESPN televised game Sept. 29, 2019

PART THREE:

Chapter 17 – The 21st Century

1. Leonard Koppett, *Koppett's Concise History of Major League Baseball*, Carol and Graf Publishers, 2004, p492

2. Statement from Rick Cerrone, *Baseball Digest*, June 2, 2020

3. Koppett, p494

4. Lisa Beamer with Ken Abraham, *Let's Roll Ordinary People, Extraordinary Courage* Tyndale House Publishers, Inc. Wheaton, Illinois, 2002, p214

5. Phone interview with Nick Sette, MLB Data Quality Analyst

6. The George J. Mitchell Report http://www.baseball-almanac.com/mitchellreport

7. Ibid.

8. Mark-Fainaru Wada and Lance Williams *Game of Shadows; Barry Bonds, BALCO, and the Steroid Scandal That Rocked Professional Sports* Gotham Books, 2006, p199

Chapter 18 – The Game

1. https://www.espn.com/mlb/story/_/id/27977973/why-did-world-series-games-last-long

2. Ibid.

3. https://www.nytimes.com/2018/08/16/sports/baseball-mlb-strike-outs.html by Tyler Kepner Aug. 18, 2018

4. https://www.weforum.org/agenda/2019/04/business-case-for-diversity-in-the-workplace/

5. Ibid.

6. https://www.mlb.com/diversity-and-inclusion/pipeline-program

7. Alyson Footer, May/June 2020 *Baseball Digest*

8. https://www.mlb.com/news March 29, 2019

9. https://www.mlb.com/international

10. By Rob Harris / The Associated Press https://www.recordonline.com/sports - May 8, 2018, at 2:00 a.m. Updated May 9, 2018 at 12:58 a.m.

11. Bob Nightengale, *USA TODAY* Published 3:39 p.m. ET June 30, 2019, | Updated 2:49 p.m. E.T. July 1, 2019

12. Ibid.

13. *The Guardian Today*,

14. Mike Ozanian, Forbes, *The State of the Game in 2019*

15. Mike Ozanian and Kurt Badenhausen of Forbes staff, *The State of the Game in 2019*

16. Ibid.

17. Sen. Henry Waxman, (D-CA Subcommittee Hearing, April 14, 1994

18. Emma Bacculieri, *Sports Illustrated*, July 23, 2018

19. https://www.nytimes.com/2020/06/24/sports/baseball/mlb-coronavirus-rules.html

20. Ibid.

21. Eve Schaenen statement, June, 2019, Executive Director, The Yogi Berra Museum and Learning Center

22. Brian Richards statement, New York Yankees Museum Curator, June 2020

Bibliography

Adelman, Melvin, *A Sporting Time; New York City and the Rise of Modern Athletics* University of Illinois Press (1986)

Adler, Jolhn, with Draper Hill, *Doomed by Cartoon; How Cartoonist Thomas Nast and The New York Times Brought down Boss Tweed and His Ring of Thieves;* Morgan James, Garden City, NY, 2008

Allen Oliver, *New York, New York;* New York MacMillan Publishing, 1990

Alexander Charles, *Our Game-An American Baseball History* Henry Holt and Company, New York, 1991

Appel, Marty, *Pinstripe, Empire*, Bloomsbury Press, 2012

Appel, Marty, *Munson: The Life and Death of a Yankee Captain*, Anchor, 2010

Babicz and Zeiler, *National Pastime; U.S. History Through Baseball* Rowan and Littlefield, 2017

Bowman, Larry, Soldiers at, Play: *Baseball on the American Frontier-for Nine: A Journal of Baseball History and Culture*

Bryson, Bill, *The Babe Didn't Point,* Iowa State University Press, 1986

Burk, Robert F., *Much More Than a Game,* The University of North Carolina Press, 2001

Crain, Esther *The Gilded Age in New York 1870-1910,* Black Dog and Leventhal Publishers, 2016

Creamer, Robert, *Baseball-and Other Matters in 1941*; First Bison Books, 1991

Czitrom, Daniel, *New York Exposed – The Gilded Age Police Scandal that Launched the Progressive Era."* Oxford University Press

Ellis, Edward Robb, *The Epic of New York City – A Narrative History –* Old Town Books, 1990

Ferber, Bill, ed, *Inventing Baseball, The 100 Greatest Games of the Nineteenth Century,* SABR, 2013

Giamatti, A. Bartlett, *Take Time for Paradise: Americans and Their Games* Summit Books, Simon & Schuster, 1989

Golenbock, Peter (2002). *Bums: An Oral History of the Brooklyn Dodgers.* Mineola, New York: Dover Publications

Golway, Terry, *Machine Made; Tammany Hall and the Creation of Modern American Politics*; W.W. Norton & Company Ltd. (2014)

Gorn, Eliot J. and Warren Goldstein, *A Brief History of American Sports; Second edition* University of Illinois Press, 2013

Graham, Frank, *The New York Giants: An Unofficial History of a Great Baseball Club,* The Southern Illinois University Press Series.

Headley, Elizabeth, *The History of New York from the Beginning of the World to the End of the Dutch Dynasty* by Diedrich Knickerbocker

Hynd, Noel, *The Giants of the Polo Grounds,* Doubleday New York, 1988

Holway John, *Josh, and Satch: The Life and Times of Josh Gibson and Satchel Paige,* Carroll & Graf Publishers, New York, 1991

Honig, Donald, *The American League, An Illustrated History*, Crown Publishers, Inc. New York 1983

Johnson, Lloyd, *Baseball's Book of Firsts*; Brompton Books (1999)

Kirsch George, *The Creation of American Team Sports;* University of Illinois Press; First Edition, 1989

Koppett, Leonard, *Major League Baseball,* Carroll & Graf Publishers, New York 2004

Morris, Peter, William J. Ryczek, Jan Finkel, Leonard Levin and Richard Malatzky *Base Ball Founders: The Clubs, Players and Cities of the Northeast That Established the Game,*

McFarland and Company, Inc., Publishers, 2013

Nemec, David, *The Beer and Whiskey League* Lyon & Burford, 1994

Newman, Roberta and Joel Rosen, *Black Baseball, Black Business-Race Enterprise and the Fate of the Segregated Dollar*; The University Press of Mississippi, 2014

Pietrusza, David, *Rothstein, The Life and Times of the Criminal Genius Who Fixed the 1919 World Series* Carroll & Graf Publishers, New York (2003)

Rader Benjamin, Baseball – A History of America's Game, 3rd ed. University of Illinois, 2008

Ed Rielly, Baseball; An Encyclopedia of Popular Culture, ABC-CLIO Inc.,

Riess, Steven, A., *City Games: The Evolution of American Urban Society and the Rise of Sports,* Illini Books Edition of the University of Illinois, 1991

Ryczek, William J. *Baseball's First Inning; A history of the National Pastime through the Civil War* McFarland and Company, 2009

Seymour, Harold, *Baseball: The Early Years* Oxford University Press, 1990

Burt Solomon, *The Baseball Timeline in Association with Major League Baseball*; DK Publishing, Inc. 2001

Stout, Glenn, *Yankees Century*, Houghton Mifflin, 2002

Sugar, Bert, *Bert Sugar's Baseball Hall of Fame; A History of America's Greatest Game* Running Press Book Publishers (2009)

Thorn, Palmer, Gershman & Pietrusza, *Total Baseball, 6th ed.*, Total Sports, New York 1999

Thorn, John, *Baseball in the Garden of Eden; The Secret History of the Early Game*; Simon and Schuster, 2011

Zoss, Joel, and John Bowman, *Diamonds in the Rough: The Untold History of Baseball*, MacMillan Publishing Company of New York, 1989

Articles and Interviews

Chapter 1

1. https://www.history.com/topics/inventions/cotton-gin-and-eli-whitney

5. https://study.com/academy/lesson/the-market-revolution-in-america-definition-lesson-quiz.html

6. https://courses.lumenlearning.com/boundless-ushistory/chapter/the-market-revolution/

9. George Thompson, *National Advocate*, April 25, 1823, page 2, column 4. "New York Baseball, 1823," The New York Times

14. http://www.19cbaseball.com/game.html

Chapter 2

6. https://courses.lumenlearning.com/boundless-ushistory/chapter/manifest-destiny/

7. https://riversprojectweek.weebly.com/impacts.html

8. Kimberly McGee s://www.theclassroom.com/political-party-opposed-idea-manifest-destiny-11585.html

9. Jonathan Kirsch, Sept. 19, 2004, https://www.latimes.com/archives/la-xpm-2004-sep-19-bk-kirsch19-story.html

10. John Thorne, https://ourgame.mlblogs.com/the-knickerbockers-san-franciscos-first-base-ball-team-part-two-bb71094011e7

Chapter 3

1. John Thorn, *Our Game*; Spring 2011 issue; https://ourgame.mlblogs.com/the-new-york-game-in-1856-6c58bdd4a420

4. Andrew Schiff, SABR – *The National Pastime Volume 28*, 2008, p26

11. Michael Beschloss, https://www.nytimes.com/2014/09/27/upshot/the-longest-game-williams-vs-amherst.html

12. https://www.ncaa.com/news/baseball/article/2019-07-01/story-first-ever-college-baseball-game-1859

13. https://en.wikipedia.org/wiki/College_baseball

14. Daniel R, Epstein, https://tht.fangraphs.com/the-stop-and-start-history-of-womens-baseball/https://en.wikipedia.org/wiki/College_baseball

15. Ibid.

16. Ellen Klages, https://www.exploratorium.edu/baseball/features/girls-of-the-summer.html

Chapter 4

6. https://constitutioncenter.org/blog/on-this-day-lincolns-emancipation-proclamation-changes-history

7. http://totallyhistory.com/enrollment-act-of-1863/

8. http://ushistoryscene.com/article/baseball-and-the-civil-war/ by ZacharyBrown,

9. https://www.loc.gov/pictures/item/94508290/

10. http://ushistoryscene.com/article/baseball-and-the-civil-war/ by ZacharyBrown,

11. Kirsch, *Baseball in Blue and Gray*, Princeton University, 2003, p124,127 12.

12. https://catto.ushistory.org/catto-and-american-civil-rights/

13. https://en.wikipedia.org/wiki/Jim_Crow_laws

15. https://fordhamsports.com/roster.aspx?rp_id=1294

16. Mitch Wojnarowicz/National Baseball Hall of Fame and Museum)

17. Telephone interview with Frank Cutrone on Aug. 9, 2020

Chapter 5

3. https://www.history.com/topics/19th-century/gilded-age

8. http://www.loc.gov/teachers/classroommaterials/presentationsandactivities/presentations/timeline/riseind/

10. https://www.baseball-reference.com/bullpen/Reserve_clause

11. Home / Sports Card News / Vintage Sports Card News / Peck and Snyder

Chapter 6

2. https://www.baseball-reference.com/bullpen/Reserve_clause 4.spalding-bros.com/it_en/storia/

8. https://www.history.com/topics/black-history/fourteenth-amendment

11. LOC, *Baseball Americana*, 2009, p35

12. Ibid.

13. https://courses.lumenlearning.com/boundless-ushistory/9/the-progressive-era/

14. https://www.britannica.com/biography/Jacob-Riis

16. https://americasfavoritepasttime.weebly.com/original/baseball-during-the-progressive-era

Part Two:

Chapter 7

4. Tony Morante, *The Baseball Research Journal*, SABR, Spring 2013, p34

9. Eddie Frierson, SABR https://sabr.org/bioproj/person/christy-mathewson/

11. https://m.facebook.com/PDNYHistoryInColor/posts/2076412322381117

Chapter 8

5. Bill Francis, https://baseballhall.org/discover/1918-flu-pandemic-didnt-spare-baseball

Chapter 10

4. www.bguthriephotos.com › keys › 2018_DC_LOC_Baseball

Chapter 11

7. https://www.aagpbl.org/history/league-history

8. https://baseballhall.org/discover-more/stories/baseball-history/league-of-women-ballplayers

11. Michael Haupert, https://eh.net/encyclopedia/the-economic-history-of-major-league-baseball/

Chapter 12

2. *The New York Times, April 16, 1947, in Sports of the Times*: Play Ball!

    In addition, Dodgers' manager, Leo Durocher was suspended for marrying actress Laraine Day, before she was divorced causing an uproar, especially in the Catholic church.

3. Ibid

4.   Louis Efrat, The *New York Times*, April 27th, 1947

11.   Sal Yvars, Giants catcher at a Westchester, NY SABR meeting

14.   Louis Effrat, *The New York Times* March 19, 1953

15.   Joseph M. Sheehan, *The New York Times*, September 30, 1953

16.   Ibid

17.   Idem

16.   https://www.scpr.org/news/2008/06/24/2554/walter-omalley-was-influential-bringing-dodgers-la/

Chapter 13

4.   https://timesmachine.nytimes.com/timesmachine/1964/08/14/issue.html

5.   Ibid.

7.   https://baseballhall.org/discover-more/stories/short-stops/pfister-papers-give-inside-look-at-mlb-draft

8.   www.mlbplayers.com

9.   Ibid.

10.   http://www.seanlahman.com/baseball-archive/brief-history-of-baseball

11.   www.mlbplayers.com

12.   Ibid.

13.   https://www.mlb.com/news/negro-leagues-celebrating-100th-anniversaryBill Ladson, Feb.14, 2020

Chapter 14

5.   Sam Roberts, *New York Times* Dec. 6, 2015 from https://sabr.org/research/turbulent-70s-steinbrenner-stadium-and-1970s-scene

7.   https://sabr.org/research/turbulent-70s-steinbrenner-stadium-and-1970s-scene

8. Ibid.

9. https://bleacherreport.com/articles/154265-come-to-think-of-it-the-day-that-changed-major-league-baseball-forever

10. Appel, *Pinstripe Empire*, p432

12. Telephone interview with Ms. Joan Gianmarino, Feb. 9, 2020

Chapter 15

6. https://www.history.com/topics/natural-disasters-and-environment/1989-san-francisco-earthquake

7. https://www.nytimes.com/1989/09/02/obituaries/giamatti-scholar-and-baseball-chief-dies-at-51.html Robert McFadden, September 2, 1989

8. https://mason.gmu.edu/~rmatz/giamatti.html

Chapter 16

5. https.//www.faithandfreedom.com/baseball-america-and-the-21st-century

6. ESPN televised game Sept. 29, 2019

Chapter 17

2. Statement from Rick Cerrone, *Baseball Digest*, June 2, 2020

5. Interview with Nick Sette, MLB Data Quality Analyst

6. The George J. Mitchell Report http://www.baseball-almanac.com/mitchellreport

7. Ibid.

Chapter 18

1. https://www.espn.com/mlb/story/_/id/27977973/why-did-world-series-games-last-long

2. Ibid.

3. https://www.nytimes.com/2018/08/16/sports/baseball-mlb-strike-outs.htmlby Tyler Kepner Aug. 18, 2018

4. https://www.weforum.org/agenda/2019/04/business-case-for-diversity-in-the-workplace/

5. ibid

6. https://www.mlb.com/diversity-and-inclusion/pipeline-program

7. Alyson Footer, May/June 2020 *Baseball Digest*

8. https://www.mlb.com/news March 29, 2019

9. https://www.mlb.com/international

10. By Rob Harris / The Associated Press https://www.recordonline.com/sports - May 8, 2018, at 2:00 a.m. Updated May 9, 2018 at 12:58 a.m.

11. Bob Nightengale, *USA TODAY* Published 3:39 p.m. ET June 30, 2019, | Updated 2:49 p.m. E.T. July 1, 2019

12. Ibid.

13. *The Guardian Today,*

14. Mike Ozanian, Forbes, *The State of the Game in 2019*

15. Mike Ozanian and Kurt Badenhausen of Forbes staff, *The State of the Game in 2019*

16. Ibid.

17. Sen. Henry Waxman, (D-CA Subcommittee Hearing, April 14, 1994

18. Emma Bacculieri, *Sports Illustrated*, July 23, 2018

19. https://www.nytimes.com/2020/06/24/sports/baseball/mlb-coronavirus-rules.html

20. Ibid.

21. Eve Schaenen statement, Executive Director, The Yogi Berra Museum and Learning Center, June 12, 2019

22. Brian Richards statement, New York Yankees Museum Curator, June 2020

Made in the USA
Monee, IL
06 April 2021